D0518784

C800500012

A LESS BORING HISTORY OF THE WORLD

A LESS BORING HISTORY OF THE WORLD

From the
Big Bang to Today

DAVE REAR

■ SQUARE PEG

LONDON

Published by Square Peg 2012

2 4 6 8 10 9 7 5 3 1

First published in Great Britain in 2012 by
Square Peg
Random House, 20 Vauxhall Bridge Road,
London SW1V 2SA

www.vintage-books.co.uk

Addresses for companies within The Random House Group Limited can be found at:
www.randomhouse.co.uk/offices.htm

The Random House Group Limited Reg. No. 954009

A CIP catalogue record for this book
is available from the British Library

ISBN 9780224087025

The Random House Group Limited supports The Forest Stewardship Council (FSC®),
the leading international forest certification organisation. Our books carrying the FSC
label areprinted on FSC® certified paper. FSC is the only forest certification scheme
endorsed by the leading environmental organisations, including Greenpeace. Our
paper procurement policy can be found at www.randomhouse.co.uk/environment

Mixed Sources
Product group from well-managed
forests and other controlled sources
www.fsc.org   Cert no. TT-COC-2139
© 1996 Forest Stewardship Council
FSC

Typeset and designed by carrdesignstudio.com
Printed and bound by Clays Ltd, St Ives PLC

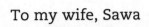

To my wife, Sawa

1. In The Beginning...
(15 BILLION–4500 BC)

Part I: The First 14.99 Billion Years   3

A Short Diary of the Big Bang: 15 billion–4.5 billion BC   3

Life on Earth: 3.5 billion BC   6

The Age of the Dinosaurs: 245 million BC   9

The Age of the Mammals: 65 million BC   13

Part II: The Evolution of Man   16

Out of the Trees: 3 million BC   16

Neanderthal Man: 300,000 BC   18

Homo Sapiens (Cro-Magnon): 30,000 BC   20

The Neolithic Era: 8000 BC   21

2. The First Civilisations
(4000–300 BC)

**Part I: How the World Got Civilised:
4000–1200 BC**   27

The First Civilisation   27

An Eye for an Eye and Other Fun Customs   31

Part II: The Egyptians: 3000–1090 BC   33

The Rise of Egypt   33

The Decline of Egypt   35

Part III: The Age of Small Nations:
1200–800 BC   38
The Phoenicians   38
The Hebrews   40

Part IV: The Age of Empires: 800–300 BC   44
The Friendly, Neighbourly Assyrians   44
The Persians   46

Part V: Meanwhile, in the rest of the world:
2500–256 BC   49
Ancient India   50
Ancient China   53
The End of the First Civilisations   55

3. Classical Civilisations
(300 BC–AD 620)

Part I: The Greeks: 3000–30 BC   59
The Trojan War and Other Greek Fantasies   59
The Rise of the Greeks   60
Alexander the Great   66

Part II: The Rise and Fall of the Roman Empire:
753 BC–AD 476   68
The Founding of Rome   68
The Punic Wars   69
The Death of the Republic   71

The First Emperors 73
The Decline and Fall of the Roman Empire 76
The Rise and Rise of Christianity 77

Part III: Classical China and Irresistible India: 256 BC–AD 618 79
The Classical Chinese 79
The Golden Age of India 82

4. The Middle Ages Outside Europe
(AD 500–1600)

Part I: The Byzantine Empire and the Rise of Russia: AD 450–1600 87
The Rise of the Byzantines 87
The Fall of the Byzantines 89
The Rise of the Ivans 91

Part II: Muslim Empires: AD 600–1500 94
The Rise of Islam 94
The Ottoman Empire 96

Part III: The Far East: AD 600–1600 98
The Moguls in India 98
The Tangs, the Songs, the Mongs and the Mings 100
Japan 101

Part IV: Africa and the Americas: AD 300–1600   104
The History of Africa   104
The Origins of North America   105
Civilisations of the Americas   107

5. The Middle Ages in Europe
(AD 500–1500)

Part I: The Dark Ages: AD 500–1000   113
The Holy Roman Empire   113
The Vikings and the Magyars   117
The Anglo-Saxons   119
Fun with Feudalism   121

Part II: The Slightly Less Dark Ages:
AD 1000–1500
The Black Death   124
The Crusades   126
England Has Real History, Kings etc.   129
The Church   136

6. Europe Has a Renaissance
(AD 1500–1763)

Part I: The Renaissance and the Reformation:
AD 1350–1600   141
The Renaissance   141
The Reformation   143

**Part II: Countries Take it in Turns to be Top Dog:
AD 1500–1750**   150

The Golden Age of Spain   150

The Golden Age of France   152

The Golden Age of Oliver Cromwell's Warts   154

**Part III: Europe Discovers the World:
AD 1492–1763**   160

The Age of Exploration   160

Empire Hunting   162

Britain Becomes Top Dog   165

7. Revolution, Baby
(AD 1700-1815)

Part I: The Age of Reason: AD 1700–1800   171

The Scientific Revolution   171

The Enlightenment   173

Enlightened Despots: Prussians and Austrians   174

Enlightened Despots: Russians   176

Part II: The Age of Revolution: AD 1763–1815   179

The American Revolution   179

The French Revolution   181

The Napoleonic Era   187

Part III: The Industrial Revolution:
AD 1750–1820   190
New Inventions   190
Dark, Satanic Yorkshire   191

8. The World Gets Obsessed by Isms
(AD 1815 - 1914)

Part I: Liberalism in Britain, France and America:
AD 1815–1914   197
The Balance of Power After Napoleon   197
Liberalism in Britain   198
Republicanism in France   200
Expansionism in the US   201

Part II: Nationalism in Italy, Germany and
Russia: AD 1815–1914   204
German Unification   204
The Crimean War   207
Independence in Latin America   208

Part III: The Age of Imperialism: AD 1815–1914   211
The Scramble for Africa   211
The Jewel in India's Passage   213
Handing Out the China   214
The US Gets an Empire, too   215

9. The World Attempts to Blow Itself Up
(AD 1914 - 1945)

Part I: The First World War: AD 1914–1918 219
The Causes of the War 219
The Course of the War 221
The Treaty of Versailles 223

Part II: The Rise of Dictators: AD 1917–1939 225
The Russian Revolution 225
The Rise of Mussolini 227
The Rise of Japan 229
The Rise of Little Adolf 230

Part III: The Second World War: AD 1939–1945 233
The Road to War 233
The War 235
The United Nations 238

10. The End of the World
(1945-PRESENT DAY)

Part I: Rocky vs Drago: AD 1945–2000 243
The Cold War 243
War in Korea 246
War in Vietnam 246
The Fall of the Soviet Union 248

Part II: Independence and Revolution: AD 1945–2000

Part II: Independence and Revolution:
AD 1945–2000   250
Independence for India   250
Problems in Africa   251
Trouble in Latin America   253
Revolution in China   255

Part III: The World Today   257
Israel and the Middle East   257
The First Gulf War   259
Palestinian Terror   260
Al-Qaeda and the Taliban   262
The Axis of Evil   263
War in Iraq   266
Financial Armageddon   267
What next?   269

1

IN THE
BEGINNING . . .
(15 billion–4500 BC.)

PART I

THE FIRST 14.99 BILLION YEARS

❧

A SHORT DIARY OF THE BIG BANG: 15 BILLION–4.5 BILLION BC

15,000,000,000 BC

alcohol units 0 (v.g), cigarettes 0 (v.v.g), waist: infinitely small!, orgasms 1 (big one)

Hurrah, have finally got underway! And gosh, feels so good to let it all hang out after being crammed into single point of infinite density for so long. Think I may have overdone it slightly in first second or so, but you can hardly blame me for getting carried away. No idea what future generations will call this momentous occasion, but do hope they come up with something original. I like Big Climax myself.

'ALCOHOL UNITS: 2; CIGARETTES: 12; WAIST: EXPANDING (SURELY ONLY TEMPORARY BLIP); GALAXIES: 1'

13,000,000,000 BC

alcohol units 2, cigarettes 12, waist: expanding (surely only temporary blip), galaxies 1

Got bit of shock today. Am not, as previously assumed, uniformly dense. It appears that in my initial enthusiasm I may have inadvertently allowed large clouds of hot gas to congregate in certain parts of my anatomy. So-o-o-o embarrassing! Shall have to wear my large pants to church tomorrow. These clouds of gas have, rather cheekily if you ask me, now begun to compress under force of own gravity. Some of them have even formed stars. Worse news: the stars have started to attract each other, and now I've a whole galaxy on my hands. (Actually, not on hands, but let's not go into that.) Desperately hoping it's just an isolated incident.

10,000,000,000 BC

alcohol units 20, cigarettes 48, waist: still expanding (let's not panic), galaxies 10^{25}

Disaster! Stars attracting each other all over the place, like some kind of gigantic singles party. Now have galaxies everywhere. It's as if have come out in huge adolescent spotty rash. *Really* horrid. No idea what to do about it. Gravity has taken over everything. Also, some of those early stars seem to be running out of fuel. Bloody hell! What next? What if they explode, like boils?

8,000,000,000 BC

alcohol units 46, cigarettes 117, waist: infinite (perhaps time to panic?), supernova 1

Holy Jehovah, supernova! What a horrible, horrible day. Everything I had feared about those stars came true. One of them blew right up in my face. Naturally, I went to see the doctor, and he told me the whole thing was bound to happen. Now he tells me! Apparently, these stars power themselves by something they call nuclear fusion, and when they run out of atoms to fuse together, they go and implode. I wouldn't mind, but they don't do it quietly. They spit out gas and all sorts. Absolutely vile. No wonder I can't get a girlfriend. The worst thing is that half of them end up as whacking great black holes, which might sound pretty cool when you say it, but wait till you get one in the middle of your navel. Not even big pants can disguise this one.

4,500,000,000 BC

alcohol units 467, cigarettes 2896, waist: Marlon Brando (!!), Earth 1

Well, the doctor got very excited today. Apparently, I've created a solar system in a galaxy he calls the Milky Way, and he thinks it's rather special. I told him, 'Doc, there's nothing special about it; I've got quintillions of them all over the shop.' He said, 'Yes, I know, but this one's going to be a bit different. I can feel it in my bones.' I said, 'You don't have any bones, Doc, you're ethereal.' But apparently he was only talking figuratively. Anyway, all he kept saying after that was, 'Wait and see! Wait and see!' Mysterious old devil. I wonder what's going to happen? Either way, I don't think it'll be as good as that planet near Alpha Centauri 12. They've invented cars already.

Diary ends.

Life on Earth: 3.5 billion BC

It only took the Earth about a billion years to form the first strands of life, which is not bad considering it takes children almost that long to put on their shoes. The surrounding solar system had coalesced into huge lumps of rock which floated aimlessly through the void. The Earth itself was created when these lumps collided with each other randomly in violent, messy explosions:

a pattern of reproduction the human race has adopted ever since. For the first billion years or so, it spent its time bubbling away as molten rock and sulphur, but eventually it cooled down into a viscous ocean of warm water and amino acids. This so-called primordial soup* contained the basic ingredients that allowed the formation of life.

The first pond life was not, as is commonly assumed, the news desk on the late, lamented *News of the World*, but minute single-celled bacteria known as prokaryotes. They fed on the molecules floating about the primordial sea, and through their metabolism produced hydrogen sulfide, a pungent gas that smells of rotten eggs. Needless to say, they found it hard to get girlfriends, and had to rely on cell division, or mitosis, for reproduction. Conversations round the soup bowls would go like this:

'Oh Jesus Christ, Jeff! Have you just metabolised in here again? Can't you just hold it in?'

'Don't you start, Peter. Mary's been going on at me all day about that. She says she wants to split up.'

'Again? How many offspring does that woman *need*?'

Like many lovelorn folk, Jeff and his prokaryote friends consoled themselves by binge soup-eating. So desperate were their love lives, however, that eventually the soup began to run short, creating massive queues at the supermarket. This became the Earth's first ecological crisis.

In response to said crisis, a new kind of cell – blue-green algae – developed, which was able to absorb light directly from the sun to make its own food. This process – photosynthesis – created oxygen as a by-product, which had the added benefit of being poisonous to stinky prokaryotes like Jeff. The slow build-up of oxygen eventually began to alter the composition of the Earth's atmosphere towards the breathable proportions of today. It also created an ozone layer, which acted as a shield to protect the Earth from the sun's powerful ultra-violet rays, eventually allowing the algae to sunbathe topless on Bondi Beach.

With the prokaryotes dying out or being forced to slink away into dark corners, there was space in the world for some new kids on the block. It took another one and a half billion years to happen, but eventually more sophisticated single-celled organisms arrived, such as amoebas, which could boast their own nuclei and chromosomes. This allowed a more complex form of mitosis, encompassing the basic biological principles of sexual reproduction, a point of not inconsiderable pride to amoebas. Then, after another billion or so years, in 650 million BC, came the first multi-cellular organisms, like worms and jellyfish.

The Earth, too, had evolved considerably, getting closer to the place we know today. There was much less volcanic activity, and the patches of land that had existed before had coalesced into two giant continents called Gondwanaland and Laurasia.* There followed a proliferation of vegetable life, and much of the land mass became covered in forests and swamp. Animals,

* So named in the 1960s when LSD was popular.

too, emerged, spiders and insects first, and later reptiles and mammals.

Then, around 250 million BC, almost everything died. Scientists are unsure exactly what caused the mass extinction, but the most recent theory has pointed the finger at a rogue volcano in Siberia, possibly secretly controlled by the Russians. Whatever the truth of the matter, over a period of a million years roughly 95 per cent of all marine life and 70 per cent of land life died out.

After four billion years of tireless evolution, the Earth was understandably disappointed by this turn of events, and briefly toyed with the idea of giving up on life altogether and taking up a career as a planet-killing asteroid instead. But, fortunately, the old blue planet was made of sturdy stuff, and soon hit back with the perfect riposte: dinosaurs.

The Age of the Dinosaurs: 245 million BC

The Age of the Dinosaurs was without doubt the single coolest time in the Earth's history, and that includes the 1966 World Cup in England. Dinosaurs were so cool in fact that, at the age of thirty-six, I still wish I was one. These mighty beasts ruled the Earth for 165 million years, which is about 164.9 million years more than humans have managed so far, and only died out when they were smacked in the face by a giant meteor. Even the way they became extinct was cool.

THE AGE OF DINOSAURS: THE SINGLE
COOLEST TIME IN THE EARTH'S HISTORY,
UP TO, AND INCLUDING, THE 1966
WORLD CUP.

Palaeontologists have discovered thousands of fossilised fragments scattered all over the world, leading them to believe there must have been millions of these fearsome creatures roaming the earth.* To explain about all of them would be long, complicated and almost as boring as, say, palaeontology. We shall, therefore, follow the lead of most reputable dinosaur experts and restrict our account to:

* Or one great big one, perhaps.

THE TOP FIVE COOLEST DINOSAURS OF ALL TIME (IN REVERSE ORDER, TO BUILD UP THE TENSION)

Coming in at Number Five is the Triceratops. The Triceratops is most notable for always (in any dinosaur book you're ever likely to pick up) being pictured fighting a Tyrannosaurus Rex. Usually, Rex is attempting to bite the Triceratops's head off, while the plucky 'Ceratopsian' is frantically stabbing its foe in the thigh with a horn. Nobody knows who won these fights, but, based on bone strength and offensive weaponry, palaeontologists have surmised that it was almost certainly either one or the other. Apart from this, we don't know much about Triceratopses, (yes, that's the plural) except that they look suspiciously like rhinoceroses (so is that), which definitely count as being among the coolest animals around today.

Making a bold entrance at Number Four is the Giganotosaurus, which, as you have possibly guessed by now, was both 'gigantic' and a 'saurus'. In fact, it is the largest meat-eating dinosaur hitherto discovered, a full four feet longer than a T.-Rex and three tonnes heavier. As if this didn't already automatically qualify it for top five coolness, it also had a banana-shaped brain. Give it up for the Giganotosaurus.

In third place comes the biggest dinosaur of all time, the Ultrasaurus. Ultrasaurus sounds like one of those names palaeontologists made up during a drunken argument about who had discovered the best dinosaur:

'Hey, guess what? I found an Ultrasaurus the other day,' boasts palaeontologist number one, getting in a round.

'Oh yeah? Well, I found a Supersaurus only yesterday,' shoots back palaeontologist number two.

'Ha, that's nothing!' chimes in a third. 'Last year, I discovered a Superdupersaurus!'

Then a fourth palaeontologist walks into the pub with a fossil the size of Manhattan and says, 'What do you think of this? I call it the Absolutelyfuckingfabusaurus', and so on . . . Despite its silly name, at a hundred feet in length and fifty feet in height, the Ultrasaurus still lays claim to being the biggest creature ever to have walked the planet. And you can't say fairer than that.

The second coolest dinosaur that ever lived is, of course, the mighty Tyrannosaurus Rex, the so-called 'tyrant king'. For a long time, the T.-Rex was held by palaeontologists to be the very pinnacle of dinosaurhood, the kind of reptile they would take into a bar with them when trying to pick up girls.* But recent controversy has weakened its claim to the throne. Critics such as Professor Jack Horner of Montana State University, in Bozeman, argue that the Rex's oversized olfactory lobes, relatively slow speed and frankly risible arms made it more suited to scavenging than hunting. Rather than being a mighty and noble killing machine, Horner dismisses the Rex as a slow, smelly, scavenging wuss. Not everybody agrees, however, and in a famous rebuttal to the Horner case, Cambridge academic Richard Metcalf in 2008 made the following statement: 'Hang on, didn't Professor Jack Horner sit in a corner eating a Christmas pie, then put in his thumb, pull out a plum, and cry "What a good boy am I"? What sort of palaeontologist does that make him?' The dispute rages on.

This brings us to Number One. After much deliberation and heartache, considering the last-minute appeals of

---

* Unsuccessfully.

many other well-known species such as the Vulcanodon and Zigongosaurus, the award for best dinosaur in a feature-length geologic era goes to . . . Deinonychus. The reason, as if we need one, is that experts believe Deinonychus was *the* most deadly dinosaur that ever lived. To quote from just one of these experts: 'Deinonychus was *the* most deadly dinosaur that ever lived.'

Deinonychus, or raptor, was fast, agile, powerful, keen of eyesight, and one of the most intelligent of all the dinosaurs. In contrast to the pathetic arms of the T.-Rex, it had three huge curved claws on each hand, as well as smaller ones on its feet. It hunted in packs, allowing it to kill even the huge sauropods. It was, in short, a monster, and way, way cooler than anything in, say:

The Age of the Mammals: 65 million BC

If the dinosaur era had been the proudest moment in Earth's history, its immediate aftermath was certainly the most embarrassing. After the dinosaurs were wiped out by the giant meteorite, the Earth was ruled for a time by – get this – large flightless birds. With most of the scary reptiles dead, scientists believe that proper birds – i.e. ones that can actually go in the air – discovered that food was now so plentiful and easy to come by that they could simply hop around on the ground until they found it. Gorging themselves stupid each day, eventually these big birds grew so fat and lazy they literally couldn't lift themselves off the ground any more, rather like Michael Moore. For twenty million sad years, this remained the case, until at long last they were forced to give way to creatures which actually did some work for a living. These new top dogs were the mammals, whose dominance has pretty much remained unrivalled to this day.

There had been several species of mammal around during the time of the dinosaurs, but only in the form of small, mouse-like creatures that spent most of their time hiding, which is presumably what they were doing when the meteorite struck. With the dinosaurs out of the equation, however, the tiny mice went out to play and seized the opportunity to start growing up and changing shape. Pretty soon, there were elephants, rhinos, lions, mammoths and sabre-toothed tigers roaming the land, not quite dinosaur scale in matters of coolness but a whole lot better than birds that couldn't even fly.

The diversification of the mammals was aided by the position of the continents, which had by now spread out into roughly those we know today. During much of the dinosaur era, there had been only one huge land mass, the ultracontinent known as Pangea ('All-Earth'), which had made early dinosaur Olympics rather one-sided affairs. Now, however, thanks to the invention of plate tectonics, the continents had separated, and evolution was free to take place more intensely in the more segregated regions of this brave new world. With the world's life forms becoming ever more divergent, even blatantly ridiculous animals like the emu found themselves a niche.

It was not all plain sailing for the mammals, however, as minor little irritations like ice ages kept interfering to wipe out species at regular intervals. The last one occurred in what is known as the Pleistocene Epoch, which, incidentally, is the only epoch in the Earth's history that children have to be warned not to put into their mouths. It lasted from 1.6 million years ago to 10,000 years ago, though it was also interspersed with interglacial periods, when the ice sheets retreated. Some geologists maintain that we are currently living through an interglacial age ourselves, citing the ice sheets that still cover Greenland and Antarctica as proof. They warn that one day in the future the glaciers could make a dramatic and destructive return, unless humanity works together now to head off this frosty catastrophe by spraying aerosols, burning fossil fuels and encouraging cattle to fart uncontrollably.

Test Yourself on the First 14.99 Billion Years

1. Discuss the popular creationist theory of 'intelligent design', with particular reference to London's transportation network.

2. Assuming the continents continue to drift, what are the odds that France will one day crash into the sun?

PART 2

THE EVOLUTION
OF MAN

ᴥ

Out of the Trees: 3 million BC

Most people nowadays agree that human beings are
descended from apes, apart from a vocal minority of
Christian fundamentalists in the American Midwest,
who appear to have evolved from emus. The transition
between ape and man occurred 3.2 million years ago at
around seven o'clock, when a precocious young apess
called Lucy decided to clamber down from her tree
and stand upright on two legs for the very first time,
promptly knocking herself out on a low-hanging branch.
This was just the first of many evolutionary mishaps
that nevertheless eventually saw groups of hairy proto-
humans scrabbling about together on the forest floor,
wondering why their ancestors kept crapping on their
heads.

A million and a half years later in Africa, they were
still at it. But by now, they had made a number of
miraculous discoveries that made their daily struggle

for survival much easier. The first of these was stone, which primitive man realised, after a great deal of trial and error, was not a kind of very hard potato which, if you just boiled it long enough, would eventually become edible. For a while the only use they could find for stones was to throw them up at the relentlessly shitting monkeys, and so primitive man did that a lot, not yet fully understanding the laws of gravity. Then they started making tools with it, earning themselves the moniker *Homo habilis*.* These tools were not much cop as hunting weapons, so their diet was generally based on fruits and nuts, which the monkeys would occasionally throw down to them out of pity.

* Literally, 'Person who spends far too much time at B&Q'.

They also discovered fire, which, again after much trial and error, they correctly worked out was not a type of clothing. Alas, as it would unfortunately be many millennia before Lord Baden-Powell formed the Scout movement, they didn't know how to actually make fire, and so they had to wait for it to occur naturally, through a lightning strike or some other form of spontaneous combustion. Then they would carry it with them wherever they went, waving it around excitedly in a stereotypical caveman-like way.

Homo habilis ruled the roost for 200,000 years, until they were finally supplanted by the proud and upstanding *Homo erectus*, a name most anthropologists still can't say without giggling. Improving their tools to include axes and knives, they were probably the first real hunters, forming hunter-gatherer societies in which the men went out to hunt for meat while the women stayed at home to gather berries and fruit. This arrangement has, of course, changed little over the passing millennia, though nowadays women can get all the meat, berries and fruit they want from Tesco, leaving them free to gather other important things, like shoes. Men, meanwhile, have become entirely superfluous.

As well as hunting, *Homo erectus* finally worked out how to make fire by painstakingly rubbing two sticks together in a pile of dry cinders until eventually swearing uncontrollably in frustration and turning to the Zip firelighters their wives had fortunately remembered to pack. This made their lives considerably more convenient, particularly as there was an ice age going on. The campfire became not only a place for cooking, but also a social occasion. The group would gather round at night to share stories of the day's hunt and activities, then later someone would bring out a guitar and start up a chorus of 'Kum Bah Yah', which was all the primitive language of the time could come up with. After a few minutes, the group would come to their senses and club him to death.

Neanderthal Man: 300,000 BC

Neanderthal man is named after the Neander Valley in Germany, where a skeleton was first unearthed in 1856. Initially, scientists believed Neanderthals to have been little more than doltish brutes with heavy clubs and beast-like features, who stomped along with limping gaits, their heads slung forward on big, squat necks. Then they realised that the skeleton they had been looking at was that of a *modern* German, and chortled mirthfully at their perfectly understandable mistake.

The Neanderthals differed significantly in physical form from other species of early man. They were taller and more powerfully built, with heavy jaws, thick eyebrow ridges and large noses. Having mastered the use of fire, they could inhabit the cold glacial regions that came with yet another ice age, hunting successfully with stone weapons and creating warm clothing from animal skins. They were also the first humans to bury their dead. They did this with a certain amount of ceremony, burying tools, weapons, food and even flowers along with the body, suggesting they may have believed in an afterlife. This was probably a good thing since their actual lives were almost certainly shit.

The Neanderthals were widespread in Europe, Asia and Africa until around 30,000 BC, when, in the grand tradition of life on Earth, they became extinct. Scientists have long been puzzled how this relatively intelligent creature could have died out. One theory proposes that they failed to survive the onset of a particularly harsh ice age; another that they succumbed to a virulent disease. A third suggests they may have married into other groups of humans, gradually ceasing to exist as a separate species, though you'd have to think those other humans must have been fairly desperate. A

nowadays women can get all the meat, berries and fruit they want from Tesco, leaving them free to gather other important things, like shoes.

fourth, less palatable, idea, is that they were wiped out by another species of man co-existing at the time, *Homo sapiens*, from whom we ourselves are descended. There is no definitive evidence for the theory, but given the bloody record of the Wise Man since 30,000 BC, it seems somehow appropriate that the history of the modern human race should have begun with genocide.

Homo Sapiens (Cro-Magnon): 30,000 BC

Homo sapiens had been around since about 70,000 BC. But by 30,000 BC, thanks to a bit of Darwinian survival of the fittest and the odd extermination of their evolutionary rivals, *Homo sapiens* was king of the hill. From their homestead in Europe, *Homo sapiens* spread all over the world, including the Americas and Australia, where they gradually devolved back to *Homo erectus*, a situation that remains to this day.

One reason we know so much about Cro-Magnon man is thanks to his fondness for scribbling on walls, a noble art form now known as vandalism. Displaying levels of delinquency that put our own modern youngsters to shame, these advanced men and women would crawl into the dim interiors of caves and then, in orgiastic fits of criminality, draw all over the walls in paint that archaeologists still now find hard to remove.

For clothing, they wore the latest fashions, which in Cro-Magnon times meant only one thing: leather.

CRO-MAGNON FASHION—SKIMPY LEATHER
NUMBERS, HELD TOGETHER PRECARIOUSLY
WITH THIN LENGTHS OF STRING.

Hardworking wives began to knock out all kinds of skimpy leather costumes, held together precariously with thin lengths of string.* Meanwhile, there was an ice age going on, meaning couples had to spend months and months crammed together indoors. These were indeed Wise Men.

* Think Raquel Welch in *The Land That Time Forgot.*

The Neolithic Era: 8000 BC

One morning in 8000 BC, Cro-Magnon man woke up early, stepped out of his sturdy tepee-style dwelling, and said: 'Er . . . darling, what did you do with all the ice?' His wife, who during the entire ice age had worn nothing but a few bits of leather held together by string, smiled for the first time in eight millennia. 'At last,' she said. 'Now I can plant my courgettes and get in the bedding plants.' She immediately began to pace out a plot, planning exactly where she was going to put the petunias, while her husband went back inside to fetch his favourite bow and arrow. He was hoping to hunt down a mammoth or deer or wild boar, or – because you never knew your luck – maybe even a late-surviving Neanderthal. 'I'm just going out, darling,' he announced breezily. 'I'll be back in time for dinner.' Only to find his wife blocking the door with a bag of John Innes compost. 'What? While there's *digging* to be done?'

The New Stone Age was greeted with dismay by men the world over. Instead of dragging themselves out of bed around mid-morning, meeting up with their mates for a quick chat about leather and string, and then popping out to kill something, husbands suddenly found themselves forced to work for a living, tending the garden and cultivating crops. One of the first telltale signs of neolithism, apart from a general air of disenchantment, was the domestication of animals. People seemed to prefer eating creatures from their own backyard to chasing around in the wild for sabre-toothed tigers, a development renowned anthropologist Richard Leakey has called 'quite gay'. Instead of being hunted for their meat, startled mammoths suddenly found themselves rounded up and forced to live in barns, leading to the first known case of a species deliberately making itself go extinct.

Soon neolithic families had moved out of their makeshift caves and huts and built houses for themselves, thus ending the semi-nomadic lifestyle of the palaeolithic era. And, because they had not thought to invent IKEA or BHS, they even had to make their own crockery, pots, storage jars and other objects far less appealing than spears and poisonous arrows. It was no fun, and for this reason people tended to die at around thirty-five, generally on purpose.

The final 'advance' made was in terms of clothing. As techniques of livestock raising and farming improved, neo-lithic people were able to produce more fibres to work with. Eventually, they learned to weave these together into cloth. This led to a whole new fashion, which, apart from a brief and ultimately embarrassing flirtation with leather pants in the 1980s, has never really looked back. Neolithic wives who dared to leave their houses still wearing their old leather tank-tops were quickly ridiculed. 'Oh my god!' people would shriek in horror. 'That is so Old Stone Age.'

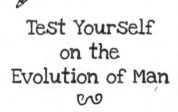

Test Yourself
on the
Evolution of Man

1. What on earth does 'Kum Bah Yah' mean anyway?

2. How about 'Oh Come All Ye Faithful'?

The world, indeed, had moved on.

2.

THE FIRST CIVILISATIONS
(4000-300 BC)

Introduction

Look up the word 'civilisation' in the dictionary and you will find something like 'an advanced human community with its own sophisticated culture and society', which seems to rule out Canada. However, a more accurate definition of the word would probably be 'an advanced human community with its own sophisticated culture and society that is quickly wiped out by another advanced human community with its own sophisticated culture and society, preferably through wholesale massacres and mass inductions into slavery, while this new advanced human community with its own sophisticated culture and society is then in turn wiped out by another advanced human community with its own sophisticated culture and society, until quite frankly nobody's really sure which advanced human community they're supposed to belong to at all, and, Christ, weren't we all just better off hunting mammoths in the Stone Age?'

PART I

HOW THE WORLD GOT CIVILISED

4000-1200 BC

෧෨

The First Civilisation

The dreariness of the neolithic revolution meant that it did not catch on everywhere at the same time. Although sunny Mesopotamia and the Middle East succumbed very early on, Central Europe managed to hold out for another three thousand years, while plucky Britain heroically hung on to its backwardness until 3000 BC. There were, therefore, significant variations in when different parts of the world became civilised.

The first of the world's true civilisations grew up in Iraq at the lower end of the Mesopotamian valley, close to where the Tigris and Euphrates empty into the Persian Gulf. Clay tablets surviving from the period refer to the king of Sumer, which seemed like a good name for the people as a whole. Over a period of over 1500 years, the Sumerians developed cities, governments, laws, calendars, temples, trade and literature, at a time when the Celts in Britain were still centuries away from mastering the art of painting themselves purple.*

The principal activity of the early Sumerians was drowning in floods. They did this successfully year after year, for they were an advanced people. But eventually some of them began to wonder if this might actually be something they would be better off *not* being successful at, and started to think of ways they could prevent it happening so much. Not living between two huge rivers that flood all the time was an idea popular for a while; lifejackets was another. Unfortunately for the Sumerians, the latter idea was scuppered by the recent invention of bronze, which tended not to float very well. So instead, they plumped for a third option: constructing a vast and complex network of dykes and irrigation canals.

This was much better, and it also had the added benefit of providing water for the fields even during the dry season. The problem was that maintaining the dykes was a lot of work, far too much for individual farmers, who still spent most of their time reminiscing about the ice age. To organise the large-scale projects needed to carry out the work, the Sumerians, displaying the same kind of perspicuity and astuteness that had led them to live in a flood zone in the first place, decided that the best thing to do would be to create something called a 'government' and leave all the organising to them. This

* As a means of making their appearance more terrifying to their enemies — as if their orange beards and incomprehensible accents weren't enough.

bold and inspirational move paid great dividends, and the Sumerian government finally brought the irrigation project to a successful completion (just 800 per cent over-budget) in AD 2002, a mere 4300 years after the Sumerians had ceased to exist.

With the well-irrigated fields producing crops in surplus, many people took the opportunity to quit farming for other professions, thereby creating a 'division of labour' that was a prerequisite for calling themselves a real civilisation. Soon Sumer was awash with carpenters, potters, metalworkers, masons, carvers, boat-builders and jewellers, and it was quite a long time before anyone realised that, owing to the fact that Sumerians lived in isolated farming villages, there wasn't actually anything for these new artisans to do. Worried about the effect of rising unemployment on its polling numbers, the Sumerian government decided to tackle the problem by building cities.

These new cities devoted their time to bettering themselves and mankind as a whole by attempting to massacre each other at regular intervals with bronze swords. In between times, they invented a calendar based on the movements of the moon, measured time using minutes and seconds, worshipped vengeful gods, condemned the world to six thousand years of language lab lessons by building the Tower of Babel, and indulged in growing amounts of trade. It was probably the latter that led to their greatest invention of all: writing. With goods leaving and entering the city storehouses in great numbers, the Sumerian government needed a way to keep track of them, because otherwise how would people know which forms they had to fill in? They came up with a kind of pictographic writing called *cuneiform* (another word historians can never say without smirking). As the number of symbols increased over time, eventually they were able to produce entire sentences, like this one:

CUNEIFORM: AS THE NUMBER OF SYMBOLS INCREASED OVER TIME, SUMERIANS COULD EVENTUALLY PRODUCE WHOLE SENTENCES, LIKE THIS ONE

Despite these achievements, however, when crunch time came, the Sumerians were found wanting. By 2500 BC, they had spent so much time warring with each other, their power over the region had weakened, and they were becoming vulnerable to attacks from rival peoples in the north. In 2300 BC, they were set upon by an Akkadian king called Sargon, who had woken up one day and decided, like Roy Castle before him, that he wanted to be a record-breaker. Consulting Norris McWhirter, who was born around this time, Sargon found that there was really only one record worth breaking in the ancient world, and that was the most-wars-in-a-single-reign record, presently held by King Urukhegal of the city of Uruk. He set about his task with dedication, because he'd heard that's what you need, and in the next fifty years managed to wipe out every city in Mesopotamia. It was all over for the trendsetting Sumerians, and within two hundred years nobody even spoke their language.

An Eye for an Eye and Other Fun Customs

The Akkadians didn't last long, unfortunately, because they happened to exist at the same time as the Babylonians, who are much more famous. In 1750 BC, the leader of the Babylonians, King Hammurabi, united all the city-states of Mesopotamia, and, in an act of typical quiet modesty, gave them a new set of laws, which he discreetly engraved on an eight-foot pillar. This so-called Code of Hammurabi was the first time laws had ever been written down, and they caused quite a bit of consternation at first as there were 282 of them and most people couldn't read. Nevertheless, once they got a feel for what the penalties were, the citizenry found it made life much simpler. Particularly as most of them were, by this time, dead. The Code of Hammurabi prescribed the death penalty for pretty much everything, including 'coveting your neighbour's livestock', 'talking too loudly in a bar' and 'surprising another man's wife'. Another part of the code famously decreed 'an eye for an eye, a tooth for a tooth', which at least cut down on dentists.

The relative stability of the Babylonian civilisation was beset by an invasion of nomadic Kassites from the East. The Babylonians hoped the Kassites would do the usual nomad thing of killing everyone they could find and then moving on. But to everyone's surprise (including, dangerously, Babylonian wives), the Kassites found they quite liked living in Mesopotamia and decided to hang around. For the next four hundred years, the Kassites distinguished themselves by somehow finding a way to do absolutely nothing useful at all. They built no temples, wrote no books, made no new inventions, enacted no draconian laws and fought no significant wars. It was a job even getting them to wash up after mealtimes. The Babylonians made several attempts to get rid of their unwanted guests, dropping subtle hints about early starts in the morning and needing to put the kids to bed, but the Kassites knew when they were on to a good thing and stubbornly refused to leave.

The Kassites ended up being annihilated by a much more active* people known as the Assyrians. But that particular story must wait a few pages, for now it is time to spin the yarn of the mysterious and, let's face it, pretty darn sexy, Egyptians.

---

* i.e.
bloodthirstily
violent.

PART II

THE EGYPTIANS

3000–1090 BC

ᵔᵔᵔ

The Rise of Egypt

The Egyptians were not a people lacking in good fortune. Besides being naturally defended from invasion by seas on one side and deserts on the other, they also had a wonderfully bountiful river, which flooded predictably each year depositing rich, fertile soils on their farmlands. It was this that provided the conditions for their early jump towards civilisation. 'All Egypt is the gift of the Nile,' wrote the Greek historian Herodotus of his travels in the country. 'What a bunch of total jammy bastards.'

The rise of Egypt as a nation began when a certain King Menes managed to unite the northern and southern halves of the country in 2850 BC. He established his capital at Memphis, which caused confusion for a while because, if Menes was the king of Memphis, what did that make Elvis? But once they had sorted it out, things went pretty well. Menes and his descendants devised a clever strategy for ensuring everyone would do what they said all the time. They told people they were gods. 'See that big ball of fire in the sky, the one that lights up the day, provides us with warmth, and gives life to this mortal world, the heavenly body we call Ra?' they would say, smirking quietly. 'That's me, that is.' And the thing is, people believed them. They also believed them when the pharaohs said that the only reason the Nile flooded each year was because they told it to, and that everyone in Egypt could attain eternal life just by doing everything the pharaohs said. It was a brilliant system and it gave the pharaohs almost unlimited authority and prestige, right up until the moment the Nile happened not to flood for some reason, in which event they were generally done away with.

To be fair to them, the pharaohs did not waste their power. With a vast country to govern, foreign enemies to fight and a burgeoning economy to regulate, the kings of Egypt did what you would expect any responsible rulers to do: they built huge pointy buildings in the desert. Almost all the pyramids were constructed during this early period, including the great pyramid of Giza, which took 100,000 men more than twenty years to complete. The pyramids, of course, housed the pharaohs' tombs, and had to be so big in order to fit their heads inside. They were filled with golden treasure that the pharaoh would take with him to the other side, and contained scary messages, like 'Death will come to those who disturb the sleep of the Pharaoh', which, if nothing else, made people knock quietly before ransacking the tombs.

With such visionary leaders at the helm, Egypt underwent a golden age in which she made stunning advances in the art of incomprehensible writing systems, bizarre looking animal gods and interesting British Museum exhibits. Although there were hiccups along the way, most notably when immigrants from Syria rather uncharitably took over the country while the Egyptians were enjoying a brief after-dinner nap, Egypt was the envy of the Middle East. After 1500 BC, she even got herself an empire, which stretched from the desert sands of Sudan to the shimmering blue sea of Palestine, causing confusion among amateur archaeologists by creating Upper Egypt (in the south) and Lower Egypt (in the north). The good times seemed destined to last forever. This, of course, made it the perfect time for:

> With such visionary leaders at the helm, Egypt underwent a golden age in which she made stunning advances in bizarre looking animal gods and interesting British Museum exhibits.

The Decline of Egypt

The Egyptian Empire brought unparalleled wealth to the country, which as usual the pharaohs elected to blow on vast temples and tombs, some of which were so big the pharaohs died several decades before they were completed. Eventually, however, the people began to tire of this profligacy, particularly as *their* tombs generally consisted of the hole they made when a giant piece of masonry fell from the temple they were being forced to build. There was much dissatisfaction. Moses even went as far as leading his Hebrew people out of the country through a mythical gap in the Red Sea.

To make matters worse, Egypt's empire was proving far more difficult to govern than it had been to conquer. Agitators from the strong Hittite kingdom in Asia Minor stirred up trouble in Syria and Palestine, actively promoting rebellion against the Egyptians with attractive slogans like, 'Don't be Uptight, Be a Hittite!' and 'Join the Hittite Empire! It's Slightly Better than Slavery'.

At this critical time, Egypt was hampered by the accession to the throne of a weak and foolish pharaoh by the name of Amenhotep. Amenhotep made only one good decision throughout his reign, which was to marry the exquisitely beautiful Queen Nefertiti, famous throughout Egypt for her cutting-edge wardrobe of see-through dresses. Understandably, however, this meant the new pharaoh was not overly interested in going off to wage long, hard campaigns against the Hittites, preferring to stay at home where he could wage long, hard campaigns of a different nature. People were so envious of him they eventually forced him to abdicate in favour of his teenage son-in-law, Tutankhamun. Alas for Tutankhamun, he died when he was only seventeen, just as he was beginning to realise why he couldn't stop staring at his mother-in-law's latest dress. 'Bloody hell, what a great fucking dress!' he was heard to mutter on his deathbed, a fateful utterance that became known as the Curse of Tut.*

---

* The Curse of Tutankhamun is said to have struck down the 1922 excavators of his tomb, all of whom, mysteriously, are now dead.

From then on, Egypt struggled to hold back the invaders at its gates. Some strong pharaohs held off the assaults, notably Ramses II, but eventually they lost their empire. After 670 BC, the Assyrians, the Persians, the Macedonians, the Romans, the Turks, the French and the British all took turns to rule, and it was not until the twentieth century that Egypt finally regained her independence.

Test Yourself on the Mesopotamian and Egyptian Civilisations
ᴄᴡᴏ

1. According to *The Guinness Book of Records*, who holds the world record for making the most successful career out of the least useful talent? (*Hint: Norris McWhirter*)

2. Comment on the rumour that at least ten members of the England football team are descended from the Kassites.

PART III

THE AGE OF SMALL NATIONS

1200-800 BC

༄

The Phoenicians

The collapse of the Egyptian empire left the Near East without a proper power centre for almost four centuries, allowing weedy, peaceful nations like the Phoenicians to prosper. The Phoenicians based their power on trade. Sailing to less developed parts of the globe, they would make fair and mutually beneficial trading deals with the local populace, in which the local populace would agree to hand over their precious metals and jewels and in return the Phoenicians would agree to supply the locals with . . . wood. It is a policy multinational trading companies still like to employ with developing nations to this day. In this way, they traded with peoples in Greece, Italy, North Africa, Spain and France. There is even evidence they made it to neolithic Britain, where their first meeting apparently went something like this:

PHOENICIANS: Hail, noble Britons! We are traders in the glittering metals of gold, silver and bronze and seek to make fair and mutually beneficial trading deals with you. Tell us, do you possess any beautiful precious metals?

BRITONS: We have some tin.

PHOENICIANS: Some what?

BRITONS: Tin.

PHOENICIANS: We're not sure what that is.

BRITONS: You know, the stuff soup comes in. We've got loads of it. Thing is, we can't get it open. Do you happen to have an opener?

PHOENICIANS: We've got to be going now.

BRITONS: But you've only just come! Stay and have supper with us. We're having black pudding.

PHOENICIANS: Balls to that!

The trade with Britain didn't last long, but fortunately that gave the Phoenicians time to do other things, like invent an alphabet. Improving on cuneiform (snigger) and hieroglyphics, they produced a twenty-two letter alphabet consisting entirely of consonants but no vowels. Because this made early editions of *Countdown* a little monotonous, the Greeks later added vowels, creating the alphabet that led, via the Romans, to the one we use today. Unfortunately, even this new alphabet did not succeed in making *Countdown* any less tedious.

The Hebrews

Originally nomads from the Arabian desert, the Hebrews had settled in lower Mesopotamia, where they enjoyed the fruits of Babylonian civilisation. In 1800 BC, however, just around the time Hammurabi was prescribing the death penalty for 'forgetting to close the door after you leave a room', they decided it might be a good time to move on. Led by their patriarch Abraham, they made their way towards the land of Canaan* in present-day Palestine, where they hoped to found their own homeland. Unfortunately, when they arrived, they were aghast to discover that there were people there already, Canaanites to be exact, who were not altogether pleased to have guests. Forced to live in the most arid parts of the land, the Hebrews busied themselves with various important activities, mostly related to starving to death.

Fleeing into Egypt, they were devastated to find that there were people there too – Egyptians this time. Despite an initial period of prosperity, when Joseph wowed the pharaoh with his technicolor dreamcoat and amazing array of song and dance moves, the Hebrews quickly found themselves back under the cosh. In 1200 BC, the twelve tribes fled the country, following Moses on what they expected would be a quick jaunt through the desert back to Canaan.

Forty years later, they began to wonder if it might have been a good idea to ask how far it was first. Things were not looking good at all, but then suddenly Moses had a revelation. Seeing his people dying helplessly in

* Or Cnn, as the Phoenicians called it.

the terrible heat, half-starved and worn down by years of subjugation and hardship, he came to an important conclusion:

'I've got it,' he declared. 'We must be God's Chosen People!'

As evidence, God sent down the Ten Commandments, in which He promised to keep the Hebrews safe from all suffering and misfortune just as long as the Hebrews worshipped the One True God and didn't do something really stupid like melt down all their possessions and venerate a golden cow instead.

'Ha ha! As if we'd do anything ridiculous like that!' laughed the Hebrews, bunching together suspiciously. 'The very idea! Ha ha ha ha!'

'Oh, for heaven's sake,' said God. 'I can see the fucking thing glinting.'

Despite this little mishap, the Hebrews did eventually reach Canaan, and scored their first significant victory in history by walking round and round the city of Jericho until the walls collapsed, probably out of boredom. Then they found themselves embroiled in another conflict, this time with the mighty Philistines, led, of course, by their fearsome seven-foot warrior, Goliath. The Hebrews were hampered by squabbling between the twelve tribes, until a strong leader emerged called Saul, who made a typically clever suggestion:

'Hey, why don't we all go back to Egypt?'

Fortunately, he was only joking, and what he really meant was: 'Why don't we all join together and fight as a united people, and I'll be king?' Plus, he knew of a brave young shepherd boy called David, who was a whiz with a slingshot.

This worked, and under the successive reigns of Saul, David and David's son Solomon, the Hebrews saw off the Philistines and made themselves the leading power in the area. Solomon built a splendid temple in Jerusalem to house the Ark of the Covenant, in which the Ten Commandments were kept.* Faithfulness to Yahweh became the very cornerstone of the Hebrew nation. Solomon in particular proved to be an extremely wise ruler. For instance, when two women came to him, both claiming to be the mother of the same child, Solomon offered to cut the baby in half. While one of the women protested vehemently, the other seemed strangely satisfied, thus proving to Solomon that, frankly, the Hebrews needed to work a bit more on their Ten Commandments.

Once Solomon died, however, things started to go wrong. Some of the Hebrews had become irritated by Solomon's constant wisecracking and baby-splitting stunts, with the result that when the great ruler passed on, so did half his kingdom. The northern part formed their own breakaway kingdom called Israel, while the southerners stayed loyal, creating Judaea.

Of the two, Judaea had marginally the more luck. While the Hebrews in Israel were conquered in 722 BC by the Assyrians and carried off wholesale into captivity (something the Assyrians did quite a lot), the Judaeans

* Just about the only place the Ten Commandments were kept, judging by David's extra-marital habits.

manfully hung on by agreeing to hand over to the Assyrians a small annual tribute, consisting of the entire wealth of every person in Judaea (another thing the Assyrians did quite a lot). Then, in 586 BC, the Chaldeans invaded and carried them all off into captivity too.

Thus endeth the first lesson of the Hebrews.

PART IV

THE AGE OF EMPIRES
800–300 BC

❧

The Friendly, Neighbourly Assyrians

The Assyrians began their existence as simple farmers tilling the soils of northern Mesopotamia, and there was nothing in their appearance that would have suggested they were going to end their existence as vicious serial killers. People used to say: 'Oh yeah, I knew an Assyrian fella once. Yeah, nice chap he was, pretty quiet, kept himself to himself, you know. Then, one day, out of the blue, he just pops round my house, and, without so much as a good morning, flays me alive and enslaves my entire family! Ha! What a character!'

Like many a serial killer, collectively the Assyrians had had an unhappy childhood. Their formative years were generally spent getting kicked around by grown-up civilisations, like the Kassites and Hittites. They were also the butts of cruel teasing at school, revolving around the ambiguity of their name:

'Hey, look, it's a Syrian!'

I'm not a Syrian. I'm Assyrian.

'That's what we said.'

No, you didn't. You said I was a Syrian.

'You are a Syrian.'

No, I'm not! I'm Assyrian!

'A Syrian?'

No! Ass . . .

Eventually, the Assyrians got so irritated with this, they formed armies. At first, they only fought wars against people that had teased them. But after a while, they saw the benefit of starting wars *before* they were teased. Preventive wars, you might say, pre-emptive strikes. Under this new 'doctrine', they found the excuse to launch raids against the Hebrews, Phoenicians and Kassites as well as assorted mountain tribes and desert nomads. Equipped with iron weapons, cavalry units and siege engines, they were an unstoppable force, particularly when they began backing up their assaults with systematic acts of bloodthirsty terror and brutality. Flaying, roasting, gouging and impaling: all in a day's work for your average Assyrian. So terrifying was their reputation that many cities chose not to fight at all, preferring to 'embrace the feet' of the assailants. The Assyrians liked to respond by giving them a good kick in the teeth.

Fortunately for the civilised world, Assyrian rule did not last forever. Oddly enough, they never succeeded in capturing the hearts and minds of the peoples they butchered, except literally, and when their military resources began to be stretched thin, the Assyrians found themselves unable to stave off rebellion. In 612 BC, the Chaldeans, who had made careful studies of Assyrian military techniques, entered the capital at Nineveh, and, in an impressive display of what they had learned, massacred every living inhabitant. The Assyrian empire collapsed in seconds, and nobody, not even the Syrians, mourned its passing.

THE PERSIANS

The Chaldeans didn't last long, as they kept getting distracted by other things, like prettifying their capital at Babylon with hanging baskets all over their gardens and attempting to say the name of their most famous king, Nebuchadnezzar II, three times in a row without spitting.

Thus it was no surprise when they were smashed to pieces in around 550 BC by the warlike Persians from Iran, whose own idea of a hanging garden was one in which mass executions took place. The Persians based their power on a unit of crack troops known as the Immortals. Having soldiers who couldn't die seemed a little unfair to the armies they fought against, particularly humble races like the Hebrews, whose own crack unit – the 'Let's Try To Survive Till Lunch-ers' – never quite made it to the dining hall. Under their king Darius the Great, they created an empire that ranged from Egypt all the way to northern India, allowing the Persians to embark upon their ambitious master plan of carpeting the entire Middle East with expensive woollen rugs.

When they weren't doing that, they were practising a monotheistic religion called Zoroastrianism, articulated in the early days by a group of camel-riding men called the Magi. The Magi spent most of their time staring up at the night sky and making remarks like, 'Hey, I could have sworn that star over there just moved! Quick, let's get our camels! Oh no, wait, sorry, I think it's a helicopter. Oh, but how about that one? Oops, no, just my finger on the lens.' They were not nearly as wise as they looked.

The Persians did a pretty decent job of ruling the world, despite their unhealthy obsession with animal stables, but it all had to come to an end eventually. The kings, like most men, spent more time trying to survive the plots of their wives and children than they did strengthening the empire. The local governors too were a pain, forever trying to pull the rug out from under the king's feet. Eventually, in a series of events that were to occur in a period of history known as Chapter Three, Alexander the Great strode in from Macedonia and conquered the whole lot in about four and a half minutes. The Persian Empire disappeared as quickly as it had arisen, but it left behind a legacy of tolerant and enlightened rule that the world would not easily forget, at least for the first week or so.

The Persians based their power on a unit of crack troops known as the Immortals. Having soldiers who couldn't die seemed a little unfair to the armies they fought against.

Test Yourself on Small Nations and Big Empires

1. What was the cultural significance of the gifts of gold, frankincense and myrrh the three Magi brought to the baby Jesus? And why are they no longer stocked by Mothercare?

2. Could I have a 'P' please, Carol?

PART V

MEANWHILE, IN THE REST OF THE WORLD

2500-256 BC

ᕙᓓ

While the Middle East was busy building and destroying civilisations, people in the rest of the world were doing what they did best, too: thanking their lucky stars they weren't living in the Middle East.* They were slowly moving towards advancement – neolithic druids in Britain, for instance, had begun dragging huge boulders into Stonehenge, though they hadn't yet figured out why – but they were still plodding along in the New Stone Age. Two countries, however, were moving along quite nicely, in the sense that they too were constantly drowning in river floods. These were ancient India and China, or, as they were known at the time, modern India and China.

* A custom that still persists today.

Ancient India

INDIA DEVELOPS COWS

Before 2500 BC, while pyramids were being built in Egypt and knocked down in Sumer, there was a highly developed civilisation in India, about which historians have been able to say with 100 per cent certainty that it no longer exists. We do not know what happened to it nor who the people were that lived there, but since they left absolutely no trace of their existence it is a pretty fair bet that it didn't end well for them.

We know a little bit more about their successors, because they were considerate enough to leave ruins. These were the Harappans, who dated back to at least 2500 BC. The two Harappan cities that have been excavated were found to have been laid out in perfect grid patterns, suggesting their rulers may have suffered from an almost chronic lack of imagination. They were, however, highly advanced. They had public baths and brick-lined sewers, and the wealthier homes had indoor bathrooms and garbage chutes. Some homes in India still do. The people based their livelihoods on farming and trade, building ships that they sailed as far as the island of Bahrain in the Persian Gulf, presumably for the tax breaks.

Unfortunately, however, the civilisation did not last. This is because the Aryan race from Central Asia had run out of cows. Or, rather, they hadn't run out of cows, they just wanted more cows and they thought the Indians might have some. Aryans loved cows. It was all they thought about, day and night. Cows cows cows. They loved cows so much that their word for war translated as 'a desire for more cows'. And they made war *a lot*. They also became strict vegetarians, which makes you wonder exactly what they wanted the cows for.

Whatever their exact motivation, the light-skinned Aryans, wooed by the sound of distant mooing, crossed the Himalayas through the Khyber Pass and entered northern India. There, they came across the clean and highly developed cities of the Harappans. 'What an amazing stroke of luck!' thought the Aryans, and promptly burned them down. The Aryans were a nomadic people and didn't like to tie themselves down in one place, in case they developed culture. They quickly overran northern India, while the natives decided to flee south, particularly when they saw what the newcomers were doing to their cows.

It took the invaders well over five hundred years to settle down, but eventually they began to see the benefit of leaving behind their old rolling stone lifestyle in favour of living in well-organised, self-governing cities. Then they remembered that they'd burned them all down half a century earlier. 'Doh!' said the Aryans. Eventually, however, they rebuilt them, enabling them to have wars. They also, as they had feared, developed culture. This turned out to be something the Aryans weren't very good at, and the result was a society that will probably go down in history as one of the worst ever created. It was known as the caste system.

> They loved cows so much that their word for war translated as 'a desire for more cows'.

The caste system was like the class system in Britain, except with much bushier beards. At the top of the pile were the Brahmans: scholars and priests whose main purpose was to take as many baths as they possibly could while ensuring that nobody else took any. Next came the warriors, who formed the government of the city-states under the leadership of the rajah. After that came the artisans and merchants of the cities, then the unlanded peasants and labourers, and finally the famous Untouchables, led by outcast actor Kevin Costner.

The caste system developed detailed rules for conduct and diet. Members of different castes could not eat together or accept food from one another. Being touched by a lower-caste member was a matter of even greater shame, requiring weeks of hard purification and bathing. This gave a real edge to playground games of tag.

THE INDIANS GET REINCARNATED

The caste system became associated with Hinduism, the dominant religion of the time. This was a fun religion characterised by a belief in karma and reincarnation. If you lived a just and moral life, you built up a store of good karma, which would enable you to be reborn as someone of a higher caste. An evil person, on the other hand, would drop down the hierarchy, and might return as a pariah, an insect, or even, in extreme cases, Noel Edmonds. This was to be avoided at all costs.

From Hinduism sprang another of the world's great religions, Buddhism. It was the inspiration of an Indian

REINCARNATION: AN EVIL PERSON MIGHT RETURN AS A PARIAH, AN INSECT, OR, IN EXTREME CASES, NOEL EDMONDS.

prince named Siddhartha, who had become disenchanted with the Hindu emphasis on ritual and sacrifices. Setting out on a quest for a simpler, purer existence, he came across four people – a sick man, an old crippled man, a corpse . . . and Paul Daniels – and was filled with infinite sorrow at the suffering humanity had to undergo. Seeking to understand the cause of this suffering and thus the means to end it, Siddhartha sat under a tree for many days in deep meditation until, in a moment of great personal discovery, an apple fell on his head. This caused Siddhartha to get up, and thus his teachings spread.

Ancient China

Some doubt exists about just when the first Chinese civilisation was founded. Archaeological records suggest that an advanced culture existed as long ago as 4000 BC, but there is no information available about who the people were or what exactly they did: a little bit like Gerald Ford, really. By 2000 BC, however, there was definitely a thriving civilisation, ruled by a long dynasty of kings. During this period, the Chinese made significant advances in bronze-working, ceramics, astronomy, medicine, acupuncture, calligraphy, slavery, torture and burying people alive. They also invented a soup made from bull testicles. They developed a strong sense of their own superiority, based mainly on the fact that they were superior to everyone else, and proudly called their country 'the Middle Kingdom'* (which is not to be confused with Tolkien's 'Middle Earth').

* Or 'the Midlands'.

Each king stayed in power as long as he enjoyed the favour of the gods, known in China as possessing the Mandate of Heaven. If the crops did well and his wars were successful, the king could rule with the support of all; in the event that they failed, however, he could face rebellion and deposition. In the most serious circumstances, he might even be forced to eat the testicle soup.

Around 1122 BC, the ruling Shang dynasty carelessly lost their Mandate of Heaven, provoking a successful rebellion by the Zhou clan. The Zhou dynasty ruled for the next eight hundred years, a record-breaking feat that earned them a visit from the ubiquitous Norris McWhirter, whom they quickly tried to bury alive, having first tried out the soup on him.

Eventually, however, they lost their Mandate, and this caused a long period of disorder and chaos as various clans fought each other for pre-eminence. This was called the Period of the Warring States, and it plunged the unfortunate people of China into 150 years of almost constant philosophy. Confucius was the main culprit, with his outlandish ideas of honest, meritocratic government and respect for the elderly. He lived from 551 to 478 BC, a period he mostly spent cultivating an enormously long moustache so that people would take him seriously. It pretty much worked and his ideas spread widely through the country, though not quite widely enough, clearly, to reach the government.

The End of the First Civilisations

The wise ideas of Confucius provided a suitably uplifting finish to the era of First Civilisations. It was a period in which *Homo sapiens* had progressed from being primitive Stone Age farmers living at the mercy of nature to sophisticated rulers and builders of cities living at the mercy of each other. Things had not always gone smoothly for the peoples of the ancient world, but there was plenty more to come from the Wise Man. The Earth was about to pass into the era of Classical Civilisations, and schoolboys everywhere were about to have to start learning Greek.

Test Yourself on the Rest of the World

1. Have you ever gone to bed with a really good-looking guy only to find when you got there that he'd lost his Mandate of Heaven?

2. Did you try to be philosophical about it?

3.

CLASSICAL CIVILISATIONS
(300 BC-AD 620)

Introduction

In 300 BC, civilisations became classical. Nobody knows quite why this happened or what it really meant, but most people agreed that it was pretty much a good thing. It sounded better than being an 'early' civilisation, and though it came with certain drawbacks, like naked wrestling, people would look back and see it as having been a golden age for mankind. This is, of course, because they had forgotten what it was really like. The four classical civilisations worth talking about are Greece, Rome, China and India, all of which created large empires so that uncivilised barbarian peoples could share in their classical sophistication by working for no money and getting whipped to death.

PART I

THE GREEKS
3000-30 BC

ꙮ

The Trojan War and Other Greek Fantasies

The early Greeks were famed mostly for their ability to breed with bulls in order to create Minotaurs, angry mythical beasts that dwelled in mazes. Many archaeologists dispute the existence of Minotaurs, despite numerous attempts to mate themselves with cows. However, they have found remains of a labyrinth on the island of Crete, which is where the most celebrated Minotaur supposedly lived (the one Theseus went after). The Minotaur shared its lair with a people known as the Minoans, the earliest known Greek civilisation.

The Minoans ended up being annihilated in 1420 BC by the Mycenaeans, inhabitants of the Greek mainland. The Mycenaeans were the current holders of the record for most consecutive vowels in their name and were worried that the Minoans might start calling themselves the Minoaeans. Despite wiping out their civilisation, they took many Minoan customs back to the mainland, including their flair for ridiculous made-up myths. This led directly to the Trojan War.

Here's what we know about the Trojan War. There was a city called Mycenae, and at one point it was led by a king called Agamemnon. There was also a city that might have been Troy, and it was destroyed around the time Homer's story suggested. There is some evidence that it was under a state of siege around the time of its destruction, but it is also possible that the city was destroyed by an earthquake. The story about a Trojan prince stealing another man's wife and then feebly offering to surrender before a shot had been fired has largely been discounted, owing to the fact that the Trojans were not French.* There is absolutely no evidence to support the story that a group of treacherous Greeks hid inside a wooden horse to get inside the walls of Troy because, frankly, Paris would have happily left the door open for them.

* The fact that the prince's name was Paris, however, was astonishingly prescient.

The Rise of the Greeks

The mythical sacking of Troy was followed by a huge party, at which, as usual, the Greeks drank themselves senseless with ouzo and retsina and smashed all the crockery. Mysterious invaders from the Black Sea called the Sea Peoples took advantage and turned out the Greek

THE SACKING OF TROY AFTER PARTY:
THE GREEKS DRANK THEMSELVES SENSELESS
WITH OUZO AND SMASHED ALL THE CROCKERY.

lights. This led to a Dark Age. When the Greeks finally switched everything back on in around 800 BC, they found that not only was their crockery in bad nick but all their cities had fallen down, too. Rubbing their heads, the repentant Greeks set about rebuilding. The Greek word for the new style of city was *polis*, and for a long time they could only have one as nobody could work out what the plural was. Once they did, however, two main cities sprung up – Athens and Sparta – which spent a third of their time fighting the Persians, a third of their time fighting each other and the rest of the time fighting themselves. Over time, both of these cities developed democracies, which came from the Greek words *kratos*, meaning 'rule by', and *demos*, meaning 'total idiots'. This still provides the inspiration for modern political systems today.

THE SPARTANS

Sparta was one of the few Greek cities that didn't spread its culture through colonisation, a fact that Greeks are grateful for even today. Spartans, in fact, were not permitted to leave their city at all in case they bumped into people who were smiling, a facial expression the Spartans did not understand. Smiling, laughing and fun in general were not allowed in Sparta, as they got in the way of more important activities, such as fighting, grimacing and running up and down steps.

Life was pretty simple for the citizens of Sparta. When children were seven years old, they were given a choice as to what they wanted to do with the rest of their lives: they could either become soldiers and devote themselves to the defence of the state, or they could become women. Those who decided to become soldiers were taken to a barracks, where they spent the next twenty years being taught by the best instructors in the land that they had obviously made the wrong choice. Military life was harsh. Spartan authorities were keen for their soldiers to grow up as manly as possible, and believed the best way to do this was to deny them clothes, sleep, women and blankets. Needless to say, homosexuality was rampant. Girls endured a similarly stringent upbringing, as they prepared themselves to be perfect wives and mothers by being very, very physically fit. Children who seemed incapable of becoming either perfect wives or perfect soldiers were put to death as babies. Few of them cried about it.

At the age of thirty, Spartan males became full citizens of the state, enabling them to participate in its electoral process. Their wives, meanwhile, ran the household, bringing up the children and disciplining the servants. Spartan servants were even worse off than their employers. They came from the ranks of the 'helots', lower-class serfs who were not permitted to become citizens of the state. They formed the bulk of the population, while the Spartan citizens worked hard to keep them in check. So fearful were they of a helot uprising that once a year the state formally declared war on them, permitting all troublemakers to be killed on the spot. This was the only time the Spartans allowed themselves to crack a smile.

As well as making war on their own servants, the Spartans also liked to fight other races, most notably the Persians under King Xerxes who for ten years after 490 BC were constantly trying to take over the Greek cities. The most famous episode in the war from the Spartan side was the story of the Brave 300, who faced down the full might of the Persian army at the pass of Thermopylae and, heavily outnumbered, were all slaughtered.

> When children were seven years old, they were given a choice about what they wanted to do with the rest of their lives: they could either become soldiers who would devote themselves to the defence of the state, or they could become women.

THE ATHENIANS

The great city of Athens developed a quite different culture, and, fortunately for the rest of Greece, this is the model most *poleis* (yup, that's the plural) chose to follow. If the Spartans were the George Foreman of ancient Greece, strong, silent and stoic, the Athenians were the

Muhammad Ali. While the Spartans bludgeoned with fists, the Athenians boxed with words.

This was reflected in their democracy. In the Spartan version, citizens could vote but not debate, and the city was held together by force. In Athens, people did nothing but debate and sometimes entire decades passed without a decision being made. On the credit side, however, they did invent the practice of ostracism, whereby each year the people could vote on which public figure they would most like to see thrown out of the city. If enough votes were cast, the unlucky fellow was sent into exile, not to return for at least ten years. It was said that, because of this sophisticated system, Athens did not suffer an Andrew Lloyd Webber musical in more than eight hundred years.

The resulting peace and quiet allowed the Athenians to indulge in a lot of culture. They wrote plays, which were either tragedies (in which everybody died) or comedies (in which everybody died but in a fairly amusing manner). They also had football-playing philosophers, like Socrates, Plato, Zico and Aristotle.

Socrates made his name by inventing the Socratic Method, which involved questioning everything anybody said, no matter how straightforward. He often had conversations like this:

ATHENIAN: Hey, Socrates, what a night I had! I met this great girl at the acropolis and we made love all . . .

SOCRATES: Ah, what makes you say this creature was a girl?

ATHENIAN: What? Well, I mean she had long hair and . . .

SOCRATES: A camel has long hair. Could it not have been a camel you made love to?

ATHENIAN: Huh? No, it was a girl. Her name was Agatha. She . . .

SOCRATES: A camel may be named Agatha. Was she, therefore, a camel?

ATHENIAN: No! Will you just listen for a second? This girl was gorgeous!

SOCRATES: As a camel is gorgeous when one is lost in the desert?

ATHENIAN: You fuckwit.

SOCRATES: Camel shagger.

Eventually, when they could bear it no longer, the Athenians put Socrates to death. His disciple Plato, however, lived on, recording his thoughts in the form of long dialogues, which he may have had with himself. Aristotle, meanwhile, was a scientist in the modern tradition, who employed observation and logic to draw conclusions about the natural world, which almost invariably turned out to be wrong.

Finally, there were mathematicians like Pythagoras, who invented right-angled triangles, and doctors like Hippocrates, who swore a lot. The Hippocratic Oath included a famous injunction against assisted suicide, a common problem in ancient Greece because of the length of their plays.

When they weren't busy eulogising or euthanising,

the Athenians too went to war with the Persians. Their greatest moment came when they defeated the Persian army at Marathon, a plain approximately twenty-six miles, three hundred and eighty-five yards away from Athens. The victorious army ordered a messenger called Pheidippides to run back to Athens to report the good news, a mission he carried out admirably before promptly dying of exhaustion. Since this was an extremely pointless and wasteful death, the Athenians decided to make it into a regular event.

Alexander the Great

Macedonia was a nondescript, barbarous region to the north of Greece – just as it is today. The sophisticated Greeks never cared to pay attention to events going on inside their squalid little neighbouring country, right up to the moment they looked out of their windows one morning and found themselves staring into the faces of a hundred thousand Macedonian foot soldiers. 'Whoops,' said the Greeks, and quickly closed the curtains.

When they opened them next, they found that the Macedonians were now being led by a new king, who went by the somewhat ominous name of Alexander the Great. Alexander began his reign in a typically understated fashion by launching a massive invasion of Asia Minor, where he had decided to prove once and for all that the Persian Immortals weren't. This achieved, he then conquered Syria and Palestine, before turning his attention to Egypt. A couple of months later, he took Assyria and Babylonia. Then he advanced through Afghanistan, Pakistan, and into India, before, in something of an unorthodox move, he allowed himself to die of typhus. It had taken twelve years, and he was thirty-three years old.

The empire he had created was the largest the ancient world had ever seen. But Alexander had taken care to rule honourably and to respect local customs, except in the places he burned down. He built cities too, at least seventy of them, though nobody could be quite sure they were not actually the same place as they were all called Alexandria. When he died, the empire broke up and was divided between Alexander's favourite breeds of spider. The Seleuicids governed Syria, the Ptolemies ruled Egypt, while the Antigonids drew the short straw and got Macedonia. The period from Alexander's death in 323 BC became known as the Hellenistic Age, as Greek culture and learning spread throughout the Middle East. Many important discoveries were made, several of which the Greeks are still aware of today.

Test Yourself on the Greeks

1. If Britain introduced the Athenian practice of ostracism, which popular presenter of Top Gear do you think would be exiled first?

2. Would ten years be enough?

(A) RICHARD HAMMOND   (B) JEREMY CLARKSON   (C) JAMES MAY

PART II

THE RISE AND FALL OF THE ROMAN EMPIRE

753 BC–AD 476

∾

The Founding of Rome

Every *Star Trek* fan knows Rome was founded in 753 BC by the Romulans and the Remans. What few of these so-called people realise, however, is that *Star Trek* IS NOT REAL. Rome was actually founded by the Etruscans, the dominant people in the country we now know as Italy. It was inhabited, however, mainly by Latins, and in 509 BC this fledgling race threw out the last Etruscan king and formed a republic.

This republic was dominated by rich patricians, whose primary purpose in life was to oppress poor people, known as plebeians. They formed a political system based on the principle that no one should have the first clue as to how it worked. Senators, tribunes, propraetors, magisters, aediles, praetors, quaestors, censors and dementors roamed the streets in vast gangs, sometimes outnumbering the people they governed by a factor of almost three to one. There were also two consuls, each of whom, for liberty's sake, had the right to veto actions by the other.*

The early Roman republic was always in crisis, owing to the number of hostile tribes around that were worried about the possible spread of Latin verbs. In response, the Romans decided to build an army. The Roman army proved to be very efficient, and it quickly managed to subdue the rest of Italy. The Romans governed their new territory wisely, offering full or partial citizenship to new allies and only very rarely succumbing to the temptation to crucify entire towns.

The Punic Wars

With the Italian boot under their feet, in 264 BC the Romans turned to the football on the end of it: Sicily. Unfortunately, this brought them into conflict with Carthage, a powerful maritime nation situated close by on the North African coast. This led to the three Punic Wars. The first few battles were not very fair, because they were fought at sea and the Romans didn't have any boats. Most legionaries ended up, as the Sicilians liked to say, then as now, sleeping with the fishes. But, never short of smarts, the clever Romans soon hit upon the

* Usually by means of a concealed knife.

idea of building boats, and this quickly led to glory.

The defeat in the first Punic War left Carthage simmering with resentment, and it wasn't long before they set out for revenge under their new leader, Hannibal. Hannibal realised that the best way to attack the Romans was not by sailing the short distance across the Mediterranean, but by marching through Spain, over the Pyrenees, past the Rhône river, through southern Gaul, over the Alps and into northern Italy with, of all things, elephants. It took everyone by surprise, not least Hannibal's soldiers, several of whom the famished general was forced to eat along the way, washed down with a nice bottle of Chianti. Still, they arrived in Italy with 26,000 troops and won a resounding victory at Cannae.*

The Romans, however, were not finished yet. They adopted hit-and-run tactics against the Carthaginian army, while also secretly invading North Africa under General Scipio. Hannibal had to rush home – over the Alps, through southern Gaul, past the Rhône etc. – and arrived back just in time to lose the Battle of Zama. The Romans imposed harsh terms in the peace treaty, which the Carthaginians peacefully agreed to abide by. This unexpected act of treachery outraged the Romans so much that they launched a third war in 146 BC, in which they levelled Carthage, sold its inhabitants into slavery and sprinkled salt on the ground to make sure nothing useful ever happened there again, rather like Stoke-on-Trent.

_____

* Yes, you can.

The Death of the Republic

Over the years, the Romans gradually extended their empire, which allowed them to do fun stuff like build roads, enslave populations and hold massive orgies with grapes. They shipped the slaves back to Italy, where they were forced to work in the fields of rich landowners before dying in childless misery and pain. This, however, led to problems with local peasants, because up until that point dying in childless misery and pain in the fields of rich landowners had been their prerogative and now there wasn't anything for them to do. They all went to Rome, where they procured new employment as an angry mob. The Senate attempted to appease the angry mob by putting on bloodthirsty shows in which innocent slaves were torn limb from limb by wild animals and gladiators were slaughtered in their thousands. It worked.

Eventually, however, the mob began to tire of simply watching bloodthirsty shows and started to put on their own, usually in the street just outside the Senate House. The unhappy senators had to call upon charismatic togas like Pompey, Crassus and Julius Caesar to sort things out. They formed a ruling triumvirate dominated by Caesar, a smooth-talking patrician with a gift for inventing calendars. After a brief consulship in 60 BC, Caesar made himself governor of Gaul, ruthlessly conquering the French but electing, quite wisely, not to ship them back to Italy. He even invaded Britain for a little while, famously declaring on Brighton beach:

'*veni, vidi, vici*'*. Though they were officially allies, the three men not very secretly hated each other, and, when Crassus died in 53 BC, the stage was set for a showdown.

* 'I came, I tried the food, I left.'

Pompey summoned Caesar back to Rome on trumped-up charges related to salad-making. Caesar obeyed the order, but brought along his army as a side dish. Having fatefully crossed the Rubicon river in northern Italy, he marched on Rome, before defeating his rival at Pharsalus and forcing him to flee to Egypt, where he was promptly murdered by Cleopatra's brother-husband, Ptolemy. This upset Caesar greatly, for if there was any murdering to do, he wanted to do it himself. He went to Egypt to punish Ptolemy, placing Cleopatra on the throne and, in a cunning side move, shagging her. He then went on a tour of the empire, hunting down Pompey's friends wherever he could find them, before finally returning to Rome in 44 BC as the undisputed heavyweight champion of the world. Making himself dictator for life, he then set about making much-needed social reforms, failing to realise it was almost 15 March (warned to 'Beware the Ides of March', Caesar, like most people then and now, had no idea what this meant), which was when Brutus and Cassius had been prophesied to murder him. '*Et tu, Brutus?*' he exclaimed as the knives went in, forgetting at this most critical time that he should have declined Brutus in the vocative.

After Caesar's death, Brutus and Cassius attempted to take power for themselves, but they did not reckon on Caesar's trusty lieutenants, Octavian and Mark

Antony (although how anyone could trust a man who spells Antony without the 'h' . . .). They defeated the conspirators at Philippi, before turning on each other. Octavian controlled the west, while Mark Antony entered into an alliance – in every sense of the word – with Cleopatra. Eventually, Octavian won the showdown battle at Actium, biting Cleopatra on the asp, and the empire was his. It was 31 BC, and the Republic was dead.

The First Emperors

Octavian devised a shrewd plan for ensuring he kept a firm grip on power: he offered to give it up. The Senate, fearing yet another civil war, rejected his offer and gave him the title Augustus, meaning 'August'. This was to distinguish him from July, a month Julius Caesar had made up. Augustus governed for fifty years, an astonishing effort considering the average life expectancy of most later emperors was about three and a half minutes (the time it took for the blood to drain out). He was a great ruler, reforming the administration of the empire, strengthening its borders, building lots of straight roads, improving the army, beautifying the capital, reviving religion, patronising culture, ameliorating the lot of the people, curbing excess and vice, bringing world peace, rescuing children from burning buildings and turning water into wine.* By the end of his reign, Rome had an empire that stretched from Western Europe to the Middle East,

> Octavian devised a shrewd plan for ensuring he kept a firm grip on power: he offered to give it up. The Senate, fearing yet another civil war, rejected his offer.

* Yes, but apart from all that, what *else* did the Romans do?

including the unruly province of Judaea where a young carpenter's son by the name of Jesus was just reaching puberty. Augustus even had the forethought to choose a successor so that civil war wouldn't break out as soon as he died. He was confident the system he had established would be sturdy enough to keep the empire strong, even in the unlikely event that Rome was ruled by a succession of sadistic mad idiots.

After Augustus's death in AD 14, Rome was ruled by a succession of sadistic mad idiots. The first of these was the emperor Caligula, not his real moniker but a fond nickname given to him as a child, meaning 'little sadistic madman'. In his short but spectacular four-year reign, Caligula bedded his three sisters, appointed his horse a senator, made it a capital crime to look at his bald patch, dragged spectators into the arena to fight lions and shagged the wife of every rich man in Rome. He was murdered in AD 41 by his own bodyguard.

CALIGULA: APPOINTED HIS HORSE AS A SENATOR.

He was followed by I Claudius (better known as Derek Jacobi), a short, slightly deformed man who foamed at the mouth when angry but somehow managed to conquer the rest of Britain, perhaps because he was the only one who could be bothered. He was poisoned to death by his wife in AD 54. Then came the best of the lot – Claudius's adopted successor Nero. Nero's father had once run over a small child in his Ferrari on the Appian Way just for fun, and his little hero was determined to make daddy proud. He liked to spend the daylight hours murdering his mother, kicking his wife to death and publicly executing his friends, and it was a constant source of frustration for Nero that it was too dark to carry on doing things like that at night. Until, with typical Roman ingenuity, he hit on the idea of burning Christians in his back garden for light. As if this wasn't clever enough, this multi-talented young man also loved to sing and recite poetry, especially his own. He would compete in contests, which were free and open to all aspiring poets who didn't mind dying for their art. Rome burned in AD 64, which the citizens blamed on Nero and Nero promptly blamed on the Christians. Public games followed, and everyone soon realised that the Christians must indeed have been responsible for the fire, as they were the ones getting eaten by the lions. Four years later, however, Nero was dead, stabbing himself in the throat after being overthrown by practically everyone.

The Decline and Fall of the Roman Empire

Despite the consistent madness of its emperors, by the close of the first century the imperial system was well and truly established, dreams of a republic long forgotten. It seemed to be the only way to bring order to the unwieldy empire. It was, therefore, an extraordinary bonus that the death of Emperor Domitian in AD 96 should usher in an age of not just one but five sane leaders in a row. It was an impossible run of luck, repeated in Italy neither before nor since.

Men like Trajan and Marcus Aurelius, and building projects like Hadrian's Wall, brought order and prosperity to the empire, as well as fewer Scottish people. Cities, roads, temples, aqueducts, bridges, tunnels, public baths and grand monuments sprang up all over Europe, many of which are still there today.

The Roman Empire, on the other hand, is quite noticeably not.

Although it took a long time for the empire to collapse completely, there were warning signs early on: looming clouds of Germanic invaders, cool mists of economic slowdown, thunderclaps of political instability. After the death in AD 192 of Marcus Aurelius, nobody could decide who should be emperor and Rome declined into years of instability and civil war. So many new emperors were proclaimed by different interest groups, sometimes three or four found themselves serving at the same time. The economy, meanwhile, was collapsing, with the value of the lira falling rapidly against the Deutschmark.

In the end, the only solution was to split the empire into two, so that at least two of the emperors could find responsible work. This, however, only served to delay the inevitable. When the Visigoths defeated the Roman legions at Adrianople in Turkey in 378, the stage was set for Western empire meltdown. Alaric the Visigoth led his army into Italy, sacking Rome in 410. Meanwhile, the Huns, under their friendly and humorous leader Attila, a real gent, laid down their towels in Gaul. More tribes like the Vandals pillaged and graffiteed their way to the capital, while the Senate sent out a hopeless final decree to its citizens: 'You're on your own'. In AD 476, the last Western emperor, touchingly named Romulus, was cast from his throne, and Odoacer the barbarian took his place.

The Rise and Rise of Christianity

As the Roman Empire slowly declined, the curious religious sect of Christianity continued to grow. Having started out as a bit of a lark, when renowned practical joker Jesus decided to command rich people to give all their possessions away to the poor just to see how they would react,* Christianity had quickly spread out from Palestine and into the wider Roman world. This was largely thanks to charismatic TV evangelists like St Paul of Tarsus, who used his status as a Roman

* Not very well, as it turned out.

citizen to carry the good news around the empire. Paul wrote long epistles to the many fledgling churches he helped establish, explaining the teachings of Jesus in an organised and comprehensible form. His final message, sent out just before his death in AD 64, became legendary:

> **@Corinthians** Big J. says love neighbour as thyself. Not in dirty way obviously :)! In Rome now. Big show at Colosseum tomorrow. I'm invited!

Despite Paul's untimely execution at the hands of Nero, Christianity continued to gather followers, its wacky brand of equality before God and everlasting life appealing to the poor put-upon citizens of the empire. In 313, it gained a massive boost when the emperor Constantine, whose mother herself was a believer, made the religion legal at last. Soon, there were bishops (or 'papas') in all the major cities, and one of these – the papa of Rome – eventually assumed authority for the whole Church. As eager missionaries set out for every corner of the globe, it wouldn't be long before the Christians were in a position to start persecuting people themselves.

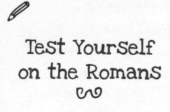

Test Yourself on the Romans

1. Brother-husband?

PART III

CLASSICAL CHINA AND IRRESISTIBLE INDIA

256 BC–AD 618

⤷⤶

The Classical Chinese

THE CHINESE BUILD A WALL

In the third century BC, there lived a little boy called Chin the Merciless. Little Chin was the teenage ruler of a large province in central China, but really he just wanted to be like all the other boys at school. But, try as he might, he simply couldn't quite fit in. His friends wondered if it had something to do with his hobby, which was massacring the inhabitants of large city-states. Whenever they tried to talk to him about it, Chin invariably lost it and wound up chopping them into small pieces with an axe. This left him with no friends at all – or a great many, depending how you looked at it. Fortunately, by this time he was the supreme ruler of all China with an empire stretching from the Gobi Desert to the South China Sea.

Little Chin did not waste his new-gained power, and devoted himself to creating a huge terracotta army that he could bury himself with after he died. He also started work on a great wall across China to keep the barbarians from Mongolia out, electing to call it, after some deliberation, the Great Wall of China. The construction was so grand that modern-day astronauts have reported that on clear nights you can look up from the wall and see space. Such hard work did not, of course, come without great sacrifice. Fortunately, Chin did not mind this, as most of the sacrifice came from peasants. It was rumoured that each brick of the wall cost a human life, pricey when you consider that nowadays most builders would charge only an arm and a leg. This led the people to give the emperor his well-known nickname: Chin the Merciless the Merciless.

The Rise of the Eunuchs

Chin was eventually deposed by the Han dynasty, which ruled China for the next four hundred years. The Hans formed the world's first government bureaucracy, a sleek organisation that at one time managed to employ more people than were actually alive in the country. The civil service was a Confucian meritocracy, having a fair and open examination that anybody of any rank could take, so long as they could write knowledgeably about the classics of Chinese literature – which naturally only the wealthiest could afford to buy.

At the top of the civil service were eunuchs, whose main role, in the absence of anything better to do, was to plot and meddle nefariously in imperial affairs. Being the only men allowed to hang around the emperor's palace of concubines, these ball-less civil servants often became the supreme ruler's most trusted advisers, a tradition that still exists today in most major democracies.

Under the Pax Sinica instituted by the Hans, the Chinese were able to make many advances in science and technology, such as papermaking, printing, clocks and sweet and sour sauce. As always, however, the wealth was concentrated in only a few hands, while the peasant masses continued to starve, drown or get worked to death in state building projects.

Eventually the Han dynasty fell, leading to three centuries of civil war. It was not until AD 589 that some order was restored, as the Sui Dynasty kicked out invading barbarians and reunited northern and southern China. In the brief time they reigned, the Suis managed to construct a great canal connecting the Yangtze and Yellow rivers. They decided to call it the Suis Canal, a clever play on words that nobody was to understand for almost fifteen hundred years. They were soon replaced by the Tangs, who didn't

---

Test Yourself on Classical China ∽

1. Name one similarity between the Great Wall of China and the idiot-savant football pundit Jimmy Hill. (*Hint: merciless chins*)

2. Have you ever secretly wondered what it might be like to be a eunuch? How about Jimmy Hill? Explain.

✔

have much of a sense of humour to begin with, and thus ended the classical era.

The Golden Age of India

India, as a big country with lots of time on its hands, continued to have a succession of important historical events, culminating in the fourth century AD when the Hindus completed a long treatise on tantric sex called the Kama Sutra. This marked the beginning of the country's Golden Age, characterised by religious tolerance, moderate taxes and lots of long lie-ins.

The rulers responsible for this transformation were the Gupta dynasty, a family of far-sighted leaders who had managed to unite the perpetually warring northern kingdoms through conquest and marriage. Through their wise governance, India became one of the most advanced nations on earth. They built hospitals, established libraries and created universities for the teaching of philosophy, art and medicine. The most famous of these, at Nalanda in the Ganges Valley, attracted five thousand students from as far away as China and Korea. Their fees were paid entirely by the Guptas, though later in the period there was a proposal to introduce a means-tested student loan system, whereby undergraduates would be expected to pay their own tuition fees by taking out low-interest loans from the Guptas repayable after a period of five years once the graduate had entered meaningful employment, provided that the annual salary they received was no less than 25,000 rupees. This was largely believed to mark the end of the Golden Age.

Of course, not everything was rosy under the Guptas. The caste system was still alive and kicking, and the number of distinct castes now ran into the thousands. Women, too, were subject to many legal restrictions. According to Guptan law, wives were expected to worship their husbands as gods.* Polygamy was common, and so was the practice of widows throwing themselves on to their husband's funeral pyre to be reunited with him in death. This practice was known as saté, whereby the unfortunate wife had to smear her body with peanut butter before joining her late husband.

* And, with the advent of tantric sex, many husbands began to think they deserved it.

Still, all in all it was a glorious time to be Indian. Indian mathematicians ruled the world, inventing trigonometry, square roots and pi. Indian astronomers discovered seven planets, calculated the diameter of the earth and developed a theory of gravity. Finally, Indian writers produced the Panchatantra, the most widely translated book in the world today after the Bible. Among its plethora of popular folk tales, it contains the adventures of Sinbad the Sailor, undoubtedly the best giant-rubber-lobster-attacks-small-foolhardy-sailor-with-suspicious-beard stories ever written.

Test Yourself on Classical India

1. Have you ever been in a bookshop furtively leafing through a copy of the Kama Sutra when a shop assistant walked past and looked straight at you? Did you end up buying *A Brief History of Time* instead? What happened when you tried to use it on your girlfriend?

4.

THE MIDDLE AGES OUTSIDE EUROPE

(AD 500-1600)

Introduction

As the Roman Empire collapsed, early medieval Europe was
sucked into a great big hole so deep it would take centuries for
them to dig their way out. Things regressed so far that at one
point it was rumoured leather shorts had come back into fashion,
until people realised it was just something the Germanic tribes
were into. In the East and beyond, however, the world was just
as bright and bonny as it ever had been. As the West forgot
everything it had ever known, the East just kept on learning,
occasionally even managing to get through an entire day without
burning down the school and slaughtering all the teachers.

PART I

THE BYZANTINE EMPIRE AND THE RISE OF RUSSIA

AD 450-1600

☙

The Rise of the Byzantines

If Emperor Constantine knew anything, it was the basic principle of real estate: location, location, elaborate home security system. Built on the Bosphorus strait, Constantinople was the link between Europe and Asia, a merchant's paradise where you could buy silk from China, spices from India and freshly dug cow dung from Western Europe. The emperor taxed it all, using the money to fortify the city and build up a powerful navy that employed a secret substance called Greek fire* to burn enemy ships.

The Byzantines had survived the Germanic invasions by using a tactic known, in technical diplomatic jargon, as

* Now thought to be a form of chilli kebab sauce.

selling your friends down the river. This involved having the following conversation each time the barbarians reached your gates:

BYZANTINES: Hello, I see you're in the mood to burn a city.
BARBARIANS: Yes, we'd like that very much.
BYZANTINES: Have you thought about going to Rome? I hear it's very flammable.
BARBARIANS: Okay.

For some reason, this tactic worked over and over again, so that while Rome burned repeatedly, Constantinople sniggered mischievously. In 527, however, the emperor Justinian came to power and thought: Wouldn't it be nice if, instead of tricking barbarians into burning Rome all the time, we went over there and did it ourselves for a change? His army agreed, and so off they popped to start a new empire. They got a bit of Egypt, then Carthage, and then took Italy, though nobody cared to find out where. Everyone was very pleased, except for one or two hostile tribes in the area, like the Lombards, the Avars, the Slavs, the Vandals, the Bulgars, the Ostrogoths, the Visigoths, and the Darren Goughs, who promptly took it all back again. Nevertheless, it was good while it lasted, and Justinian celebrated his success by writing the Justinian Code, a sizzling blockbuster of a novel, a real page-turner that topped the bestsellers for centuries afterwards, owing to the fact it was the law.

Other than trade and military conquest, what really

drove the Byzantine empire was religion – lots and lots of religion. Christianity was the tipple of choice. However, it was not the same brand as in Rome because of important theological differences related to icons. Should churches have religious paintings in them or shouldn't they? How about statues and sculptures? Wallpaper? Laura Ashley furniture fittings? Emperor Leo III of Byzantium was an iconoclast and thought they shouldn't, while the Pope in Rome thought they should. The dispute raged for a century, until the Byzantines compromised by allowing people to respect icons but not venerate them, which is apparently what God had wanted in the first place. The damage with Rome was done, however. The Byzantine patriarch was excommunicated, a painful procedure before the use of anaesthetics, and in 1054 the schism was complete: Roman Catholic Church (favourite language: Latin) in the West; Orthodox Church (favourite language: Greek) in the East.

The Fall of the Byzantines

The Byzantine Empire reached its zenith in the reign of Basil II in the early eleventh century. Basil II, one of the most inoffensively named bloodthirsty tyrants in history, devoted himself to the expansion of the empire. His most notable act was to capture 15,000 Bulgar soldiers in battle and blind 99 out of every 100 of them, leaving the remainder blind in only one eye so they could lead their comrades back home. The plan did not work out well, however, for the unfortunate Bulgars, who got lost on the way and found themselves in Bulgaria and have been trying to find the way out ever since.

After Basil's reign, however, it was all downhill for the Byzantines. In Central Asia, Muslim Turks were forming and no amount of subtle posturing towards Rome was going to save Constantinople this time. A series of devastating attacks followed, forcing the emperor to appeal to the Western Church for help.

Unhappy as the Church was with the Byzantines, it was a lot more unhappy with the Muslims, and in 1095 the glorious Crusades were launched. In rode the brave knights in their red garters and immediately launched a devastating attack on Constantinople, routing the Byzantine army. 'No, no!' shouted the fleeing Byzantines, desperately. 'You're supposed to be saving Constantinople and routing the Turkish army!' 'Whoops,' said the crusaders, and quickly switched sides. But in the Fourth Crusade, they got confused again and, before the Byzantines could point out their misunderstanding, burned Constantinople to the ground. They then compounded their error by staying there for fifty years and forming their own Latin kingdom, before the Byzantines, really upset by this time, finally reasserted themselves in 1261. None of this helped the schism at all.

The Muslim Turks, meanwhile, had been laughing so hard during all this that they allowed themselves to be conquered by other Muslim Turks, who then attacked Constantinople themselves. These new Turks called themselves Ottoman Turks, after their famous leader Otto the Man Turk. In 1453, they surrounded the city and, in an act of cruel deception, used cannons to blow it up. The Byzantine Empire collapsed in a heap, and the Ottomans took control.

The Rise of the Ivans

The rise of Russia began with the city of Kiev, ruled in the late tenth century by Vladimir the Great. Kiev was pagan at this time, but Vlad the Great* had the idea that believing in the power of rivers and trees was silly and that, rather, people should entrust their destinies to an omniscient, invisible being residing somewhere in space. The question was: which invisible being should he go for? Looking around the neighbouring states for inspiration, his eye fell on Islam first. He liked the idea of having his own harem, until the Muslims told him they weren't allowed to drink alcohol, which would have been an impossible situation for a Russian. Next he flirted with Judaism. But when he started to gather together nice Jewish girls for his harem, they spoiled it by insisting on bringing their mothers along. In the end, he took the advice of the nearby Byzantine Empire and plumped for Christianity, a safer option all round. He called his brand Russian Orthodox in order to differentiate it from Greek Orthodox†, and under him

* Not to be confused with the later Vlad the Impaler, or the modern Vlad the Vostok.

† And Russian roulette

Kiev became very holy and prosperous, especially for the boyar class who ruled the city, if not quite so for the serfs, who generally just worked and then died.

Unfortunately, there were Mongols on the way, and, boy, were they in a bad mood. Actually, they might have been in a good mood: it was difficult to tell with Mongols. Either way, carefully organised into hordes, they swept across the Russian steppes in 1237, burning treasure, looting women and molesting cities like there was no tomorrow, which there wasn't if you were Russian. By about twelve o'clock, they had conquered the lot and were about to go on into Western Europe, until their general, Batu, realised it was lunchtime, which he always liked to spend in Mongolia. The rest hung around, however, and set up a capital on the River Volga.

The Mongols, however, didn't reckon on the city of Moscow, which just at that moment chose to start rising. There was an ancient by-law in Moscow which decreed that all city rulers, regardless of their real name, had to be called Ivan. Thus, it came as a surprise to no one that the rise of Moscow began under Ivan I. Over time, as the Mongols began to spend less time ruling and more time slowly pickling themselves to death in fortified goat milk, Moscow grew in power. In 1462 a new Ivan came to power, and people suspected immediately that he was going to be a great ruler, as his name was Ivan the Great. In 1480, he overthrew the Mongols, united various city-states and emerged as the first ruler of independent Russia. He began referring to himself as czar, an old Russian word meaning 'zar'.

He was succeeded by his grandson, who put people on their guard straightaway by calling himself Ivan the Terrible. He was just a child when he inherited the throne, and was forced to watch helplessly as the ruling boyars fought each other desperately for power, butchering political rivals in the palace, sadistically torturing their opponents and bloodily executing anyone who stood in their way. Except, of course, young Ivan liked watching things like that. As a ruler, he expanded Russia's borders, opened up Siberia for settlement, established trade with the West and broke the power of the boyars. The czar's other hobbies included reading books, attending mass, hunting deer, impaling farmers, roasting villagers, torturing nobles, raping women, knocking down old people, killing his son and banging his head on the ground. He set the tone for Russian rulers for centuries to come.

Test Yourself on the Byzantines and the Russians

1. List the following Russian monarchs in their correct order: Ivan the Great, Ivan the Terrible, Ivan the Monstrous, Ivan the Lendl, Ivan the Ivan.

2. What is the correct number to call if you find an iconoclast in your house?

PART II

MUSLIM EMPIRES
AD 600–1500

ॐ

The Rise of Islam

In around AD 570, a boy by the name of Muhammad was born in the hot, desolate desert of Arabia. Surrounded by burning sands, stinging scorpions, inedible lizards and hostile Bedouin, it wasn't long before Muhammad turned to religion. The Arabs at the time had a polytheistic religion centred around worshipping stones, one of which – a big black one – was kept in a cubic temple in Mecca on the Red Sea coast. Muhammad, however, had a vision in which the archangel Gabriel ordered him to preach the word of Allah, the one true God. The rulers of Mecca promptly drove the prophet out of the city, fearing that his anti-stonist stance would discourage tourists. As it transpired, Muhammad wasn't anti-stonist at all, believing that the stone had actually fallen from heaven in the time of Adam and Eve. He soon made a successful comeback, converting most of the Bedouin tribes in the region and setting the new fun religion of Islam on its way.

The enthusiastic converts of Islam decided it was important to spread the good news to other places. There were, of course, two ways they could accomplish this. The first way involved sending scholarly missionaries to meet and talk with these foreign peoples and peacefully persuade them of the great goodness and infinite mercy of the true God, Allah. Or, alternatively, they could just ride in with big curvy swords and conquer them. The Arabs chose the latter method. They turned out to be very skilled at this, and in twenty-five years they swept through Palestine, Syria, Armenia, Mesopotamia, Persia, Egypt, North Africa and part of India. Fifty years after that, they defeated the Visigoths to take Spain and created a powerful navy, thus turning the Mediterranean into a Muslim lake.

Centred around the caliphate of Baghdad, the Muslim Empire precipitated a golden age of Islam that would last for over five hundred years. The only sour note was the bitter division between Sunnis and Shiites, which was based on the inability of anyone except Shiites and Sunnis to tell them apart. The Sunnis* believed that the caliphs should be chosen by consensus, as tribal leaders had been in Arabia. But the Shiites,† on the other hand, argued that only the descendants of the prophet Muhammad had the spiritual authority to rule. Nowadays, of course, there are no caliphs of Islam, and so the Sunnis and Shiites just argue. Despite

* Or possibly the Shiites.

† Sunnis?

this unfortunate schism, the Muslim world was at least united by the common tongue of Arabic. This facilitated the spread of knowledge throughout the empire, helping the Muslims lead the world in the study of philosophy, medicine, astronomy, mathematics, navigation and polygamy.

The Ottoman Empire

As the first millennium drew to a close, Arab influence in the Muslim Empire declined, leading to a widespread outbreak of Turks. Having moved in from Central Asia and converting to Islam in the process, the Turks decided to have a bash at taking over the Middle East. This triggered the Crusades.

For the next two hundred years, the eastern Mediterranean was awash with Arabs, Byzantines, Turks and crusaders, all murdering each other desperately on behalf of a merciful God. From their capital at Constantinople, the Ottoman sultans ruled in Islamic fashion, imposing Muhammad's laws on its Muslim population but allowing Christians and Jews to live relatively unmolested. Many of their subjects chose not to convert to Islam, possibly out of fear of having more than one wife. The Ottomans defended their empire with young Christian boys who were taken into special schools and trained to become Muslim super-warriors. They were called Janissaries, and became some of Europe's finest religiously confused troops.

These were the strengths of the Ottomans. But the Ottoman Empire would not have been the Ottoman Empire without significant weaknesses, for without them it could not reach its ultimate ambition of becoming the sick man of Europe, with accompanying health benefits. Its main weaknesses were: (1) its antiquated agricultural methods, (2) its uncanny similarity to the Byzantine Empire, which had already collapsed, (3) its obsession with collective male bathing, and (4) its large number of weaknesses. Although they would stay in power for quite some time yet, the Ottomans would decline over the centuries, and eventually not even MFI would keep them in stock.

Test Yourself on Muslim Empires
ಲ೧

1. Complete the following limerick:

There was a caliph in Baghdad,
Who had weapons that made 'em all mad.
We launched a quick war,
So he'd have them no more,
Only to find we'd been ...

PART III

THE FAR EAST

AD 600–1600

❧

The Moguls in India

After various ups and downs following the Golden Age of the Guptas, the Indians made a comeback under the leadership of the gentlemanly Rajputs. The Rajputs believed they were descendants of heaven, though modern scholarship puts their origins slightly closer to Turkestan. They were a chivalrous people, who believed combat was a form of art. Fair play, respect for the enemy, no sledging of the opposition batsmen: these were the hallmarks of the Rajputs. Naturally, this made them absolutely hopeless at war, and so, when a real enemy turned up in 1200, in the form of Muslim Turks, they quickly succumbed.

From 1200 to 1400, the Turks ruled unopposed, forming a dynasty known as the Delhi Sultanate. The Delhis were not the sweetest sultanas on the vine. While the Muslims had traditionally been tolerant towards Christians and Jews, they did not extend the same courtesy to Hindus. Hindus believed in many gods, Muslims just one; Hindus used music in ceremonies, Muslims did not; Hindus worshipped cows, Muslims ate them. The most spectacular sultan was Muhammad Tughluq, who ruled from 1325. As well as murdering his father and forcing a rebel family to eat their own nephew, he once ordered the complete evacuation of Delhi, forcing its inhabitants to march six hundred miles to a new capital, which – get this – hadn't actually been built yet! 'Tugh luq,' said the unrepentant sultan.

Then, in 1526, the Mongols decided to invade. There were only 12,000 of them and they called themselves Moguls instead of Mongols, but the Indians were not to be fooled and surrendered immediately. The Moguls were led by Barbur the Tiger, so called because of his fondness for being tickled behind the ears, and he ruled in a way that shocked even the long-suffering inhabitants of Delhi. *He didn't kill anyone.* To make matters even more confusing, neither did his successors.

By 1658, the Moguls had ruled for 130 years, and nobody in India had died at all. Religions were being tolerated, art and culture was being encouraged, child marriage and widow suicide had been outlawed, taxes were low, the crime rate was down, inflation was under control, the NHS was in good order, the deficit had been cut, the Taj Mahal had been built and India was practically reunited. And the curry was delicious.

The Moguls were led by Barbur the Tiger, so called because of his fondness for being tickled behind the ears.

The Tangs, the Songs, the Mongs and the Mings

The Tang dynasty ruled the Chinese Empire for three hundred years until 906, when the last emperor was murdered by one of his generals. Fifty years of civil war followed, with rulers coming and going like concubines. With nothing going right and the people oppressed and hungry, the country was clearly in need of a song. Fortunately, there was a whole dynasty of them just around the corner. Grabbing the microphone in 960, the Songs largely carried on the good work of the Tangs, adding street lights, fire departments, restaurants, orphanages, old people's homes and a weekly Top 40 countdown to their burgeoning cities.

The only thing they weren't good at was fighting the Mongol tribes north of the border, the one solution they could think of to the problem being to pay them huge amounts of money not to invade. This worked quite well for a while, until eventually the barbarians made a simple but crucial discovery: there wasn't actually anything to buy in Mongolia. In 1206 Genghis Khan, making his first appearance on the international stage, swept down from the north, ploughed straight through the Great Wall and conquered the whole of China in a matter of seconds. His grandson Kublai carried on the good work, creating a prosperous and well-run dynasty in Beijing (or Peking, as it used to be known, duckies) that lasted until 1382. Europeans like Marco Polo came to visit him, and returned to Venice with wild tales of paper money, coal heaters and streets not made of water.

Despite this, the Chinese never really cared for the Mongols. They had the fanciful idea that the invaders smelled, even though the khans insisted that their people wash quite regularly.* In 1368, the locals eventually rebelled, overcoming the reeking Mongs and replacing them with the fragrant Mings.

* Once every four to five hundred years.

With a huge nation to reunite, northern borders to secure and a discontented peasantry to pacify, the Mings set about making priceless vases as quickly as they could. It was time China started living up to its name. To accomplish this effectively, it first had to get rid of all the Mongols, who had an irritating tendency to smash any pottery they came across. Then they fumigated the palace. After that, they sorted out their borders. In fact, for two centuries, the merciful Mings ruled well, until they panicked and realised it was high time they let the country fall into chaos. A clan of Manchus eventually took advantage of the situation, defeating the Mings through the superior droopiness of their moustaches. They would rule all the way till 1911 when the Japanese decided to pay them a visit.

Japan

Japan, a small country in East Asia, had actually been having history for a long time, but since it generally kept itself to itself, nobody had really noticed. It had its first emperor by around AD 300, a warm-hearted fellow by the name of Sujin who was, modestly, descended from the sun. He formed a dynasty that has ruled Japan ever since, claiming divine ancestry right up until 1945 when the Japanese finally realised their emperor couldn't be descended from the sun because the Americans had told them he wasn't. Reverence for the emperor formed one of the twin pillars of Japanese society, the other being Shinto, a religion that worshipped trees, flowers, stones and high-schoolgirl pornography. They borrowed their culture heavily from China, but always gave it a unique Japanese twist so that they could sell it smaller and with greater reliability.

The emperor was often only nominally in charge of the country, the real work being done by powerful clans, who spent all of their time at war with each other. They had to do this in order to give work to their samurai, who would otherwise be walking around with those great long swords for nothing. The samurai's job was to die for his lord at any and all costs. If he was unable to die on the battlefield, he had to die in his backyard by slitting his belly open by his own hand. The lord didn't really mind which he chose, just as long he didn't live to tell the tale. It became known as *bushido*, literally 'the way of the idiot'.

In the Middle Ages, several of these clans fought for supremacy: the Tairas, the Minamotos, the Hondas, the Nintendo Wiis. In 1192, the Minamotos defeated the Tairas in a big battle and won Japan as a prize.

Minamoto Yoritomo gave himself the ancient title of shogun.* His warriors got into Zen Buddhism, because it allowed them to sit in uncomfortable positions for long periods without talking. His relatives ruled until 1318, at one point seeing off Kublai Khan and the Mongols by means of a divine wind (or kamikaze) that blew their ships off course. After this, however, there was a long stretch of disunity, until a warlord named Tokugawa Ieyasu unified the country in 1600. He moved his capital to Tokyo, and ruled uninterrupted for the next 250 years. After letting in a few Portuguese Christians early on as a kind of sport, he spent the rest of the time hunting them down and torturing them cruelly, before finally putting a big sign on the coast of Japan, which said 'No Vacancies'. On a clear day, passing ships might sometimes be lucky enough to see a Portuguese missionary nailed to it.

* Literally, 'cool-sounding ancient title'.

Test Yourself on the Far East

1. Which of the following forms of suicide was most popular with the samurai: *hara-kiri, kamikaze,* or *teppan-yaki*?

PART IV

AFRICA AND THE AMERICAS

AD 300-1600

∾

The History of Africa

If early Western historians were to be believed, the history of Africa went something like this:

4.5 billion BC: Earth forms.

2 million BC: Man emerges from the trees.

200,000 BC: Homo Erectus discovers the use of fire.

AD 1871: Livingstone meets Stanley.

AD 1960: Africans start to rule themselves.

The truth of the matter, however, is that Africa had quite a bit of history in between those dates, some of it pretty good. The prosperity of the African continent was largely based around traipsing back and forth across the massive expanse of the burning Saharan desert carrying, of all things, salt. Occasionally this enabled them to form ridiculous made-up cities where the trade routes crossed, such as Timbuktu. Timbuktu, despite the stubborn refusal of most people to believe it existed, became a thriving city in the Middle Ages and an important centre of Muslim learning. Along with gold and salt, it developed bookselling as a major source of income. The Justinian Code still did as well as ever, and there was talk of a movie. It was the capital of the most powerful of the West African empires, the Songhai, who dominated the region until the late sixteenth century.

The Songhai were finally brought down in 1591 by the Moroccans who cheated by using guns. Other kingdoms continued, nevertheless, to thrive. The Kanem-Bornu mined copper and rode around on chain-mail horses. The Oba built walled cities and organised its army into legions. The Yoruba sculpted with gold and bronze, and went around shouting 'Yoruuuu—ba! We're the Yoruuuu—ba!' at each other because they liked the sound of the word.

All of these great kingdoms would, of course, be decimated by slavery in the coming centuries, and people would happily forget they ever existed. Which brings us nicely on to:

The Origins of North America

Although Stone Age man began his slow migration out of Africa as early as 1.5 million BC, it was a long time before he finally made the trip to America. 'I mean, have you ever been there?' families would gossip around the campfire. 'The people are so goddamn friendly all the time! It's like an entire nation of Ant and Decs.' In the end, the government was forced to finance a land bridge from Siberia to Alaska, offering new immigrants attractive relocation packages such as free insurance, dental care and bison. They managed to get just enough of them across before the bridge collapsed, because of illegal scrimping on the building materials. The unfortunate immigrants found themselves with no choice but to stay indefinitely, as there was no return transport due until 1492.

Slowly and desultorily, the settlers made their way down south. The more optimistic of them hung around in Alaska in the hope that the bridge would soon be repaired. They called themselves Eskimos. The others divided themselves up into Great Plains Indians who hunted bison, Northwest Indians who fished and made totem poles, Great Basin Indians who trapped small game and attempted to get parts in cowboy films, Eastern Woodland Indians who did a bit of everything, and East Coast Indians, who mainly became lawyers. They lived in a variety of dwellings, including wigwams, tepees, longhouses and wickiups, and gave themselves comical sounding names, like Crazy Horse, Sitting Bull, Pocahontas and Little Red Riding Hood. Strangely, despite the two thousand languages known to have been spoken by the different tribes, all the names were in English.

Apart from that, little is known about the history of the various tribes. Some were warlike, some were peaceful; some were nomadic, some were static; some were led by women, some by men; some were primitive, some sophisticated. In fact, the only thing that the Indians of North America did have in common with each other is that none of them were Indians.

Civilisations of the Americas

MAYANS

The Mayans made their home in the jungles of southern Mexico, Guatemala and Honduras. For six hundred years until AD 900, they slashed and burned trees, grew maize, built cities, and constructed massive pyramids like El Castillo with 365 steps. Sometimes they sacrificed people on top of them for fun. Amazingly, they did all this without metal tools, which you couldn't buy in Central America, leading many archaeologists to surmise that the Mayan people must have had very sharp hands. If this wasn't enough, they also developed a sophisticated calendar that told them exactly when the next lunar and solar eclipses were going to take place. This was very important, because without it they would have had no way of knowing precisely when the next lunar and solar eclipses were going to take place, which would have been very upsetting for the Mayans indeed.

After AD 900, however, the Mayans inexplicably abandoned their homeland and moved north, carelessly bumping into the Toltec people on the way. The Toltecs, despite having very little ability to predict solar eclipses, promptly wiped out the Mayans, leaving the future history of the Americas open to the much more glamorous:

AZTECS AND INCAS

If there was one thing the Aztecs and the Incas found more irritating than anything else, it was the inability of people to remember which was which.

'Look, it's quite simple,' the Aztecs would say. 'We're the ones who were wiped out in about five minutes by Cortés and his small band of Spanish conquistadors.'

'I thought that was the Incas.'

'No! They were wiped out in about five minutes by Pizarro and *his* small band of Spanish conquistadors.'

'Ah, that's because the halfwit Incas somehow managed to mistake a bunch of half-starved, unwashed Spanish sailors for gods, right?'

'Er . . . no, that was us.'

Okay. So were you the vile, sadistic, inhuman monsters that carried out human sacrifices, ripping out the still-beating hearts of tens of thousands of innocent men and women in a single day?'

'Now you're getting it!'

Actually, human sacrifice was important to both cultures, but, while the Peruvian Incas generally only sacrificed children, the Mexican Aztecs were willing to sacrifice anyone and anything that happened to be in the vicinity. They needed to do this in order to appease their great god Quetzalcoatl, who was a bit short-tempered. According to legend, Quetzalcoatl had once lived with the Aztecs, bringing with him gifts that would change their society forever, such as maize and pyramids. When Cortés arrived with his conquistadors, the Aztecs naturally assumed he was the reincarnation of their benefactor, returning as legend had foretold. In this, however, they were only half right, because, although Cortés was certainly a bit short-tempered, the only gifts he brought to the Aztecs were venereal disease, smallpox and slavery.

Further south among the high peaks of the Andes, the Incas built their civilisation around gold, which they worshipped as the 'teardrops of the sun'. So much gold was discovered by the Spanish invaders that a rumour grew up about an entire city constructed of the precious metal. This became known as the legend of El Dorado, which has fascinated adventurers ever since. Although few people nowadays believe that El Dorado ever truly existed, one or two individuals actually claimed they once saw it on BBC1 in 1992, and that Jesse Birdsall may have been in it. Their claims have, however, met with official denial from the BBC, and it is widely assumed the individuals must have been insane.

* Such as going a bit too far with your llama domestication.

Apart from being indirectly responsible for embarrassing soap operas, the Incas also built networks of roads, constructed mountain fortresses, performed brain surgery, domesticated llamas and adhered to a criminal justice system which prescribed the death penalty for absolutely everything.* They had no prisons, for there was no need for them, and no wheels because they weren't invented. This made it very difficult for the Incas to learn to drive.

To the Spanish, the most notable aspect of their downfall was that it was achieved with the help of a local tribe called the Wankas, whom Pizarro cleverly won over to his side with promises of Coldplay concert tickets, souped-up Ford Fiestas and endless conversations about how great their new iPhone is. The Wankas helped Pizarro kidnap and murder the Inca king Atahualpa, which was all that was necessary to send the sensitive Incas into meltdown.

Test Yourself on Africa and the Americas
〜

1. Did Dr Doolittle with his two-headed llama or did he do too much?

5.

THE MIDDLE AGES IN EUROPE
(AD 500 - 1500)

Introduction

When we think of the medieval period, we tend to imagine stinking, muddy villages, poor, oppressed serfs, dank, terrible dungeons, marauding, heartless invaders and callous, dim-witted kings. This is an entirely accurate picture. Despite the best endeavours of historians who try to tell us that, despite incessant wars, plagues, inquisitions and Bad King John, the Middle Ages were actually a time of transition when the West began to build towards the modern, prosperous era, let us remember the Middle Ages for what they were: damp, crap and far, far too long.

PART I

THE DARK AGES
AD 500 - 1000

ᕙᖳ

The Holy Roman Empire
CLOVIS THE FRANK (OR IS IT FRANK THE CLOVIS?)

This was the situation at the fall of the Roman Empire. Germanic tribes, composed mainly of goths and vandals, were tearing through Western Europe, laying waste to her cities, setting fire to buildings and forcing everybody to sing loud, really annoying drinking songs. Dark days indeed. Eventually, however, they found some nice land to farm and settled down to form kingdoms, most of which lasted almost long enough for the tribespeople to finish pitching their tents. This is because Germanic tribes were much better at destroying each other's kingdoms than they were at building their own, and preferred it that way, too. One kingdom, however, did quite well. This was the tribe in the north of Gaul who called themselves the Franks.

The Franks had a leader called Clovis, who was a

step up from the other Germanic kings in the sense that he possessed no morals whatsoever. This made him perfect for Gaul, which, after all, was just another name for France. Clovis fell in love with a Christian woman, whose condition for marrying someone with such a palpably silly name was for him to get baptised. He duly did so and thus became a man of God. The rest of the Franks also mysteriously became men of God too, and the Pope in Rome was very happy because the Franks were in control of the whole of Gaul.

Alas, poor Clovis died in 511, and he was succeeded by a procession of what could perhaps best be described as 'other Franks'. The other Franks, however, were not really into being kings, preferring the varied pleasures of life in sixth-century Gaul, such as eating dung and drowning in bogs. The real ruling was done by the chief stewards of the palace, or 'mayors'. In 732, one of these mayors, Charles 'the Hammer' Martel, defeated Muslim invaders at the Battle of Tours, forcing the Moors back into Spain and thus saving Western Europe from centuries of technological advancement and knowledge. This made the Pope in Rome even happier, and he invited the next mayor, Charles's son Pepin 'the Spanner' Martel, into Italy to dispose of some Lombards who were irritating him. Pepin duly obliged, and quickly defeated the irritating Lombards.

The Pope, now ecstatic, crowned Pepin king of the Franks, which came as a bit of a shock to the *actual* king of the Franks, who promptly drowned in a bog. In return,

> Clovis fell in love with a Christian woman, whose condition for marrying someone with such a palpably silly name was for him to get baptised.

Pepin awarded the Pope central Italy, henceforth to be known as the Papal States. It was an important moment, for the Pope had now claimed the right to crown and legitimise monarchs: quite a neat little weapon to have in your arsenal. From then on, he resolved to do it as often as possible.

CHARLEMAGNE THE SUPER-FRANK

Pepin was succeeded by his son, Charlemagne, who immediately made clear his ambition to become the most powerful leader in Europe by having a mother called Bertha of the Big Foot. Spurred on by his mother's enormous extremity, he fought sixty campaigns in thirty years, defeating the Saxons in northern Germany, the Lombards in Italy and the Avars in Central Europe.

Whenever he did this, he encouraged the spread of Christianity. He did this by offering the people he conquered a simple choice: either they could accept salvation through baptism into the Catholic faith, or they could go to heaven a little sooner than they might have planned. The Pope in Rome watched his activities carefully and was by this time so happy he was in severe danger of staining his cassock. He had been trying out his new crowning power as often as he could, and, having successfully crowned his cat, his horse and a palace gardener named Tom, was keen to add Charlemagne to his list. He invited him to a mass at St Peter's in 800, and, while Charlemagne was innocently holding his hand out for communion, quickly slipped a crown on his head, calling him the Emperor of the Romans.

Charlemagne's first thought was, 'Don't you mean Emperor of the Franks?', because, quite frankly, most of the Romans had fled town centuries ago. But, on further reflection, leader of the Holy Roman Empire sounded pretty cool, so he decided to go with it. Then, in rather untimely fashion, he died.

His descendants quickly set out to destroy the empire their father had painstakingly created. His son, Louis the Pious – a nickname they gave to kings who never did any work – started to let things slip. Then his three sons,* following traditional Germanic custom, engaged in a civil war to decide who should take over. It was settled three years later, in 843, with the following solution. First, they divided the empire into three, so that each could take one share. Then they divided each of those shares into two to make them easier to manage. After that, they split those smaller shares into more shares, before dividing those shares into yet smaller ones, until by around 880 each king was ruling an area roughly the size of a lego brick.

What the three brothers should have been doing, of course, was uniting, because, all in all, this was not an easy time for early medieval Europe. The Holy Roman Empire was not only disintegrating from within, it was also being assailed from without. For the late 800s saw a series of invasions that made the ones in the 400s seem like Bridlington tourist hordes. Vikings and Magyars

---

* He wasn't *that* pious.

were sweeping through, and they weren't there just for
the novelty ice creams.

The Vikings and the Magyars

Of all the invaders to threaten the peaceable folk of Europe,
the Vikings were the most feared. This was because of the
terrifying length of their sagas. Impoverished villagers
from Ireland to Italy would see the approach of their
fast, slick longboats, watch as the fearsome Norsemen
leaped ashore, their swords and battle-axes glinting in
the autumn rain, and think, 'Christ, they're not going to
tell us that interminable story about Beowulf again, are
they?' But the Norsemen did, as they always did, because
they were ruthless and uncaring and Danish.

THE VIKINGS: FEARED THROUGHOUT EUROPE
FOR THE TERRIFYING LENGTH OF THEIR SAGAS

Why did the Vikings leave their homes in Norway, Sweden and Denmark at all? That is a question that has puzzled historians for centuries, though not, significantly, historians who have actually tried living in Norway, Sweden and Denmark. Whatever the exact reason, the Vikings found they quite enjoyed tripping around Europe and so they did it a lot, generally equipped with lighters. They went to England, which frustrated them repeatedly by being too damp to ignite, as well as Ireland, France, Italy, Russia, Iceland, Greenland, and even Alaska. Sometimes, they would just murder everyone and leave, while at other times they would stay and start farming, trading and telling stories. People preferred it when they did the former.

* And sometimes, confusingly, 4-5-1.

The Vikings loved to fight, almost as much as they loved to put on girls' clothing and call themselves Vicky. Led by terrifying chieftains, like Eric the Red and Sven-Göran Erikksson, they fought in a 4-4-2* formation and valued their weapons so much they gave them names, such as 'leg-biter', 'hole-maker' and 'why didn't he just play a proper holding midfielder for Christ's sake?'. People didn't like them because they were pagans not Christians. Instead of Jesus Christ, they worshipped Odin, Thor and Loki, and looked forward to everlasting life in Valhalla, recently discovered to be a small village just outside Bury St Edmunds.

Together with their silly gods and overactive horns, the Vikings terrorised Europe for two centuries, before tailing off their activities around the turn of the millennium. This is because by then they had begun to accept some of the mainland's customs, such as shaking hands with people upon first meeting rather than the traditional Viking greeting of head-slicing. They even accepted Christianity, seeing in the stories and myths of the Old Testament sagas that were almost as rambling and interminable as their own.

They were only rivalled in the mayhem they created by the Magyars, nomads from the Russian steppes who had got lost and found themselves in Germany. Using hit-and-run tactics, their mounted warriors launched attacks on every village that hadn't already been burned down by the Vikings, sometimes riding for seven or eight months at a stretch before they found one. To certain four-hundred-year-old Europeans, their unruly behaviour seemed kind of reminiscent of the Huns, and they began to call them 'Hungarians', meaning 'people who seem kind of reminiscent of the Huns'. Eventually, after about fifty years of unholy raids, the Magyars settled back into their base in Eastern Europe and became Christians. Their country became known as Hungary, meaning 'country which seems kind of reminiscent of someone who's missed breakfast'.

The Anglo-Saxons

After the Romans left Britain in the early fifth century, citing poor weather and substandard public services, Germanic tribes invaded from the mainland. Landing on the south and east coasts, successive waves of Angles and Saxons inundated the countryside, pushing existing tribes, like the Celts, further and further east, eventually all the way into Wales. This still causes bitterness today. The Saxons soon came to dominate the Angles, forcing them into inhospitable and incomprehensible places like Yorkshire. But as a consolation prize they gave them the right to decide the name of the country. They were probably presuming the Angles would do the obvious thing and call it 'Anglo-Saxonland' or something of that nature, but the acute Angles knew an opportunity when they saw it and named it England, literally 'land of the Eng'. The country was eventually divided up into various kingdoms, the most important of which was Wessex, in the south. The king of Wessex, was kind of regarded as the king of England, at least by the king of Wessex if by nobody else.

The kings of Wessex had a law that stated that only people whose names began with 'E' could inherit the kingdom. Thus, England was forced to labour under the rule of Egbert, Ethelwolf, Ethelbald, Ethelbert, Ethelred, EthelSkinner etc., until in 871 the country was thrown into turmoil by the accession of someone called Alfred. Fortunately, he was the Alfred of Alfred the Great fame, which was a good job because just at that moment the Vikings, or Danes as they were euphemistically called in England, were attacking in their longboats. Some of these were the infamous 'berserks', who loved battle so much they did it naked. So Alfred did the sensible thing

> ❝ The kings of Wessex had a law that stated that only people whose names began with 'E' could inherit the kingdom. ❞

and paid them a huge sum of money to go away until he had got a proper army and navy together. This done, he then attacked and made war for the next ten years.

Eventually, in 886, the Danes sued for peace, under the terms of which they got a nice chunk of land in the north, where they could live under their own Danelaw, and in return England didn't get burned so much. It was a good deal, and it gave Alfred time to do other things, like start the Anglo-Saxon Chronicle and get confused in people's minds with King Arthur. He also helped to spread Christianity, and thus initiated a dangerous period in which England gradually became overrun by saints.

Despite Alfred's success, however, after his death in 899 Wessex immediately went back to the policy of choosing kings whose names began with 'E'. Edward, Ethelson, Edmund, Edwig, Egghead and Edwina Curry duly followed. Then came the accession of someone called Ethelred the Unready. This was very serious news, because, by an awful coincidence, the Danes had suddenly decided they wanted to take over the country again. 'No no, you can't,' cried Ethelred, who had just got up. 'I'm not — '. But it was too late.

Fun with Feudalism

The situation in tenth-century Europe was pretty desperate. Towns and cities had crumbled into dust; roads and bridges were in disrepair; bandits roamed freely about the land; people were suffering and starving;

warfare was incessant; and there hadn't been anything good on TV for four hundred years. Clearly, something needed to be done. The solution Western Europe came up with was feudalism.

Here's how it worked. In the absence of a strong central government, power was concentrated in the hands of local nobles, who controlled the land around them and commanded the loyalty of a band of knights. These mounted warriors pledged themselves as vassals to the lord, while the lord himself might pledge himself a vassal to some larger landowner, like a king. This was fine as far as it went, but it could get pretty complicated, as there was nothing to stop a knight from becoming a vassal of more than one lord. If these lords happened to have a quarrel, he would be confused about which side to fight on, and, in extreme cases, might even be forced to attack himself. This was very difficult to do while riding a horse.

Nevertheless, it offered people a measure of security, and, more importantly, gave nobles the opportunity to invent chivalry. This was the medieval attempt to make warfare a bit more polite: to butcher people, yes by all means, but also to write songs about it later. Thus, if you captured a fellow knight in battle, you didn't immediately take him down to the dungeon and slowly crush his vassals with a pair of red-hot pincers; you treated him like a guest and entertained him with self-penned songs on your lute, until he was ready to crush his own vassals with red-hot pincers. You also fell in love with every innocent maiden you saw, and did gentlemanly things like charge at three thousand enemy soldiers single-handed to show how insane you were. In the unlikely event that you survived, you then lived the rest of your life according to sound Christian principles, and never told a lie or married anyone above the age of twelve.

As well as fighting battles, lords also had to take care of their land. Fiefs were divided up into manors. Serfs cultivated the land of the manor, spending four days a week on their own plots and three days a week on their lord's. It was a harsh life, pretty much spent working, but at least it was secure. As long as the crops did not fail, serfs could have their daily meal of bread, eggs and beer, and live safe in the knowledge that they would be dead by the age of forty. The other peasants on the manor were freemen who rented their land from the lord. They included skilled workers like blacksmiths, millers, coopers and carpenters: people necessary to keep the manor functioning and self-sufficient. Later, they sold themselves on the open market as surnames.

Test Yourself on the Dark Ages ∾

1. Discuss the difference between Danelaw, canon law, common law and Denis Law with reference to the FA Cup final of 1963.

2. 'They've Gone And Dane It Again!' So went the front page headline in the *Anglo-Saxon Chronicle* when the Vikings invaded for a second time in AD 991. But what was the headline in 880 when Alfred found the Holy Grail?

PART II

THE SLIGHTLY LESS DARK AGES

AD 1000-1500

౭ఎ

The Black Death

In AD 1000, most people were pretty much convinced the world was going to end. But when it survived, without so much as an abacus glitch, they decided to celebrate with an economic revival. With the Viking and Magyar invasions over by 950, Europe was finally free to indulge in a bit of free-market economics. First, agriculture improved with the introduction of three-field crop rotation and then trade developed with the more prosperous empires of the East. Since the roads of Western Europe were still constructed primarily from dead peasants, most of this was across the sea. The principal beneficiaries were Italian ports like Venice and Genoa, though later northern Europe joined in the fun, with Flanders becoming the centre of a thriving mud industry.

Towns and cities began to spring up, encouraging a gradual exodus from the manors as people searched for a better life. On the whole, these urban pioneers found that their new lives were, if not necessarily better, then at least shorter. Towns were filthy and overcrowded, the streets swarming with sewage, rats, thieves and travelling jugglers. They were also, of course, excellent breeding grounds for epidemics.

There didn't seem anything unusual about the merchant ship that pulled into Genoa's harbour on its return from the Black Sea in 1347, except perhaps that the rats seemed a little itchier than usual. But in the next two years, one third of Western Europe's population was wiped out. The Black Death had a mortality rate of around 80 per cent, with people rarely surviving more

CITY-DWELLERS ENJOYING THE NEW SPORT OF CORPSE THROWING, INVENTED FOR THE 1348 COMMONWEALTH GAMES.

than a few days. As their communities died and whole cities were laid waste, the only consolation for people was the invention of a new sport called corpse throwing, which involved flinging pus-ridden family members into a large cart moving past at speed.

Not surprisingly, there were serious effects on the economy. The wool industry declined as the bottom fell out of the clothes market, and people were not buying as many pension plans either. On the positive side, towns were not as crowded as before and, thank God, a lot of the jugglers were killed off. Serfdom also went into decline, as lords realised it was more profitable to rent their land to peasants rather than force their old dead serfs to till it. However, on the whole the Black Death was not a positive development for Europe, and it would be more than a century before people were confident enough to start eating rats again.

The Crusades

In the 600s, Arab Muslims had had the temerity to conquer the Holy Land. They had lived there peaceably with Christians and Jews, allowing pilgrims from the West to come and pay their respects in the homeland of Jesus. But in the 1000s, Seljuk Turks, hereafter to be referred to as The Evil Infidels, took over. They immediately began brutally murdering and torturing innocent Christians, in the sense that they occasionally charged them tolls to enter Jerusalem. Pope Urban II was not going to stand for it, and when the Byzantine emperor appealed to him for help against the Turks, he called together a big meeting in France to gather volunteers for a holy war.

There was no shortage of takers. Nobles were inspired by the idea of plundering* the Holy Land, while common soldiers often joined up to escape debt, poverty or prison. Shouting 'God wills it!', this ragtag army of around 30,000 soldiers tramped across Europe to Constantinople, where the Byzantine emperor was waiting. The noble emperor looked out across the vast armies of Christ, and, seeing them bristling with determination and godly zeal, turned to his vizier and said: 'Oh shit.' The truth was, he hadn't been expecting quite so many to show up, and the idea of 30,000 plundering criminals marching across his empire was not what he had understood by the word help. He weighed up his options carefully and, remembering the proud history of his ancestors, decided there was really only one thing he could do:

'Erm . . . have you thought about going to Rome?' he suggested.

But the crusaders were too canny to fall for that old trick, and they marched straight past him into Asia Minor. This was where he got his own back a bit, because, in their haste to get to the Holy Land, the knights had forgotten that Jerusalem was not actually in Asia Minor but was a good deal further east. Having neglected to bring food or water with them, they began dropping in the heat, while squabbling desperately over everything they managed to plunder. If the Turks had

* Sorry, I mean, liberating.

had any sense at all, they would have attacked them now, but it was a hot day and they didn't quite get round to it. Instead, the crusaders somehow got all the way to Jerusalem, which they then laid siege to. After a short battle, they defeated the Turkish defenders and, seeing their chance to finally liberate* the holy city, massacred everyone inside, Muslims, Christians and Jews alike. 'God wills it!' they shouted joyously.

Eventually, however, the Turks reasserted themselves, and by the middle of the twelfth century had recaptured Edessa, not far from Jerusalem. Many of the crusaders had returned to Europe by this time, but in 1147 they heeded the call for a Second Crusade. Two armies headed by the king of France and the Holy Roman Emperor rushed to Palestine, fought each other and then rushed back, leaving the Turks happy if slightly bemused.

In 1187, under their new leader Saladin, the Muslims duly took Jerusalem, slaughtering the Knights Templar in the process. Pope Urban II, now more than 150 years old, ordered a Third Crusade of the Three Kings, and after some hunting round, Richard 'the Lion-Heart' of England, Frederick 'Barbarossa' of the Holy Roman Empire and Philip 'the Second' of France agreed to join. On the way there, Frederick Barbarossa, who had been bickering constantly with Richard over who had the best nickname, apparently had second thoughts about the expedition and drowned. King Philip, meanwhile, who didn't like Richard much either, waited until the English king had fallen asleep one night, and then, very

---

* plunder

slowly and quietly, slipped back to Europe and seized his lands in France. This left Richard to fight the Turks by himself, because quite frankly his soldiers didn't care for him a great deal either. Over the next three years, he fought Saladin's troops single-handed, and, remarkably, made no significant gains whatsoever. In the end, however, he managed to negotiate a truce, whereby the Muslims would keep control of Jerusalem but Christians would be able to visit it whenever they wanted – pretty much the situation they had been in before the Crusades started. This was known as making 'peace with honour'.

Pope Urban II, however, was not satisfied, and more Crusades followed. They culminated in the Children's Crusade, possibly the West's darkest moment, when 30,000 French school kids, led by a first-grader called Stephen and armed only with erasers, tried to launch their own assault on Jerusalem. They got as far as Marseilles, where they were tricked into boarding Muslim slave ships and were never seen again. More desultory efforts took place later, but in 1291 the last Christian stronghold, in Acre, was taken, and Pope Urban II finally died in disgust.

England Has Real History, Kings etc.

THE EVIL NORMANS

As Ethelred the Unready faffed about in his pyjamas, the Danes rapidly reconquered the country, and in

1016 placed the first real king of England on the throne. His name was King Canute, and England was his third kingdom, along with Denmark and Norway. As far as canutes went, the king was a good one, and the Anglo-Saxons were content to let the Danes rule as long as he stayed alive and on the throne. Unfortunately, he proved incapable of doing this, and he was succeeded by his sons, who were lesser canutes by far. By 1042, they had been kicked out, along with most of their countrymen, and a real Englishman* was given the hot seat. His name was Edward the Confessor, though he later claimed he was coerced.

* i.e. he was German

Edward was a pious man and founded Westminster Abbey, but eight days after it was finished, he died. He hadn't done it on purpose, of course, but nevertheless he admitted it was his fault. The king had never really been a ladies' man, if you catch my drift, and did not leave any heirs. He was succeeded by Harold the Saxon, a Saxon, but since the year was now 1066 he clearly wasn't going to be a Saxon for very much longer. William of Normandy claimed England belonged to him, on account of having visited it once as a child, and he quickly transported himself to a village in the south of England called the Battle of Hastings, where he began feverish work on the Bayeux tapestry. Meanwhile, Harold the Saxon was rushing down from Stamford Bridge, where England had been playing at home to Norway, and he arrived at Hastings just in time for William to look up from his work and stab him in the eye with a knitting needle.

The new king imposed feudalism on his new country, except that, instead of the land belonging to the nobles, William now declared it all belonged to him. To prove it, he had a book written which listed everything everybody owned, only of course they didn't own it any more, he did. It was called Domesday Book, because people felt it would be easier to escape God's wrath on Judgment Day than it would to spell the word doom properly. The king gave away some of his newfound possessions to his Norman friends, who from then on became known as barons, on account of their great French wickedness.

HENRY AND THE BECKET

The next interesting thing that happened in England was Henry II. Born in the French province of Anjou in 1133, he had married the formidable Eleanor of Aquitaine and realised that invading England was the only way he could get away from her. He spent much of his reign reforming the judicial system, something few kings had bothered much about before. Instead of deciding trials entirely by random – the old system – he introduced twelve-man juries to listen to evidence and from now on any witnesses swore to tell the truth and nothing but the truth.

This brought him into conflict with the Archbishop of Canterbury, Thomas 'a' Becket, who believed that the truth should only be told in trials with ordinary people and not ones with priests. This prompted Henry

Edward was a pious man and founded Westminster Abbey, but eight days after it was finished, he died.

to say in a jocular tone, 'Oh, I love this guy, I hope he lives to be a hundred!' upon which the archbishop was immediately murdered. Henry was then forced to spend the rest of his reign apologising to the Pope and doing penance by crawling to Canterbury on his hands and knees and beating himself bloody with birch twigs, until eventually – some said – he started to enjoy it. He also went to Ireland, again as a penance.

EVIL KING JOHN

Henry II was succeeded by his son Richard the Lion-Heart, who immediately left to join the Crusade against Aladdin. Having spent three years in the Holy Lands, he managed to get himself kidnapped by the Duke of Austria on the way back, and spent a year or so in prison. After England had paid a princely 100,000 pounds to get him released, Richard finally returned to his kingdom. The country was mightily relieved to see him, since Richard's evil deformed brother John had been busily usurping the throne in his absence. Richard promised to sort everything out, just as soon as he got back from a very quick trip to France. Naturally, nobody ever saw him again.

This left John in total charge, and he took full advantage of it over the next fifteen years by being extremely mean and oppressive and deformed. Finally, in 1215 the barons decided they had had enough and forced him to sign the Magna Carta, a historic and groundbreaking document which ordered John to:

1. Stop being so mean and oppressive and, if possible, deformed.
2. Create a Great Council to collaboratively think up ever more sinister and inventive ways to tax poor people.
3. Stop making any more excruciatingly bad films about Robin Hood.

THE HUNDRED YEARS' WAR

After the death of John in 1216, the subsequent kings of England devoted their entire reigns to attempting to ignore the Magna Carta. There were two ways you could do this as a medieval monarch: (1) Invade France so the barons would forget about democratic representation and, hopefully, get impaled on an axe, or (2) Pretend you couldn't read Latin. Edward III chose the French route.

France had been having quite a bit of history of her own during the past three hundred years, but the most important point was that the French king – who, by law, had to be called either Charles or, preferably, Louis – had no land or money, having blown most of it on full-length suits of armour designed to protect himself from hordes of angry wives and mistresses. The English king, in fact, owned more land in France than the French king, particularly after Henry II's marriage to Eleanor of Aquitaine. This is why the French resorted to dirty, underhand tactics like sneaking back early from the Crusades to take it all back. This, allied to Edward III's claim that he was actually the rightful king of

1453: A LONE SOLDIER DEFENDS ONE OF THE FEW REMAINING ENGLISH STRONGHOLDS.

France owing to the fact that he quite liked garlic bread, was a recipe for war.

From then on, the domestic reputation of each English and French king depended entirely upon their success or failure in the war, regardless of anything else that might happen. Even the Black Death paled in comparison. In 1348, for example, Edward III won a minor skirmish outside the walls of Calais, while the plague wiped out a third of England's population. People would look back later and say: '1348? Oh, now that was a *great* year!' They were confusing times.

England's early success was based on the longbow, an absurdly simple weapon that for some reason the French could never get the hang of. Victory at Crécy in 1346 was followed by more success at Poitiers, and suddenly Edward III owned half of France. But then, just as things were looking up, he became senile and the gains were lost. His successor, the mean Richard II, negotiated a valuable twenty-eight-year truce, for which he was duly deposed in 1399. He also faced a Peasants' Revolt in 1381 under the leadership of Wat Tyler, which ended in bloodshed at Smithfield when the unwitting Tyler kept replying 'Wat?' every time the king asked his name.

Richard was followed by Henry IV Parts I and II, neither of which did anything interesting. He was succeeded by Bluff King Hal, whose real name turned out to be Henry V. Henry V was, of course, the best king ever, by virtue of inventing the two-fingered salute, which he gave to the French each time he met them. This was a reference to the middle two fingers used for drawing back the string of the longbow, which the French used to cut off when they captured English archers. It is still common as a greeting today when people unexpectedly encounter Frenchmen. It was enough to give the English a famous victory at Agincourt in 1415, and Henry V wisely elected to die a few years later before people could realise it was a fluke.

After that, however, it was all downhill. In 1429, England hit its lowest point ever when it was foolhardy enough to get into a fight with a girl, Joan of Arc, which it inevitably lost. Although Joan was subsequently burned for heresy (she claimed to have heard divine voices in her head, the usual qualification needed for sainthood), she inspired the French to greatness, and by 1453 the English had been driven from every French possession except a few hypermarkets near Calais docks. This

* In the sense
that he thought
he was a tree.

coincided with a period when the English king, Henry VI, went insane,* and so the war came to an ignominious end. Technically, the French would claim they had won it, but it is also important not to forget that there is every chance they cheated.

The Church

If there was one thing you couldn't ignore in the late Middle Ages, it was the Church. It was everywhere, on practically every street corner. With its Romanesque ceilings and Gothic arches, it dominated the medieval landscape as the one institution that all the people of Europe shared, other than serfdom and the Black Death.

The Church enforced its teachings by persuading people to have faith in the one true Lord God who spoke through His representative on Earth, His Holiness the Pope; and when that failed, it just called in the Spanish Inquisition. The Spanish Inquisition began after the downfall of the Muslim Moors in the late 1400s, and its first target was the Jews. The Moors had always tolerated the Jewish minority, but when the Christians had returned to power under Ferdinand and Isabella, the Jews had done the sensible thing and started going to church, eating pork, praising the risen Christ etc. But the new Spanish Inquisition suspected that the cunning Jews were actually only pretending to be Christians and that underneath they were, in fact, still Jews. This turned out to be correct, as the Jews readily admitted once they had been tortured long enough. They also readily admitted to copulating with the devil, eating stillborn babies, having sex with llamas and being four-legged chickens. Just as we thought, said the wily Spanish Inquisition.

Once it had finished with the Jews, the Spanish Inquisition dealt with other dangerous elements in medieval society, such as heretics, agnostics and old women with warts. They were helped in this new crusade by the Dominicans, just one of literally thousands of monastic orders that had sprung up in the period. Other orders included the Benedictines, the Cluniacs and the Franciscan friars, impoverished medieval mendicants who lived on nothing but what they could beg and yet, somehow, always managed to end up grossly overweight.

This is not to say the Church was without its problems. Most serious of all was the papal schism, created in 1378 when the French and the Italians, for reasons of managerial efficiency, decided they each needed their own pope. The French pope, Clement, went to live in Avignon while the Italian pope, Urban, stayed in Rome. This was a confusing situation for everyone, not least God, and so in 1409 the Council of Pisa was called to resolve it. After much deliberation and possibly even praying, the council decided to depose the two existing popes and elect a third one. Unfortunately, they neglected to inform Urban and Clement, who refused to accede to the new pope and thus left the Church with not one but three chaps calling themselves pope. It was said that there were so many popes in Pisa at this time, in fact, that the tower began to lean. In 1417, another meeting was held, this time in a building with securer foundations, and all three popes were deposed in favour of a fourth one, Martin. This was allowed to stand, but discontent with papal authority continued. It would not happen for a little while yet, but the seeds of the Reformation had been sown.

Test Yourself on the Slightly Less Dark Ages

1. What exactly is a Becket anyway?

2. Which was most threatening to the common people of the Late Middle Ages: the Bubonic Plague, the Spanish Inquisition, or Eleanor of Aquitaine?

6.

EUROPE HAS A RENAISSANCE

(AD 1500-1763)

Introduction

In the Middle Ages, Western Europe had not been highly regarded among the world's civilisations. It was, in fact, something of a joke. The Muslims mocked its feeble attempts to wipe out their religion: 'Hey, the crusaders are coming!' they would warn each other jovially. 'Try not to laugh at their armour.' The Chinese, who by this time were driving cars and planning their first expedition to Mars, were even harsher:

How many Europeans does it take to change a lightbulb?

None. They're still using candles! Ha ha ha!

But all that was about to change. The Renaissance was spreading from Italy. New technologies were revolutionising culture and warfare. Leonardo da Vinci was inventing the helicopter. Trade was reaching new heights, and explorers were discovering there was a whole new world out there for them to destroy. Europe was on the rise, and civilisations everywhere were going to tumble down the incline.

PART I

THE RENAISSANCE AND THE REFORMATION

AD 1350-1600

෧෨

The Renaissance

The Renaissance began in Italy during the late fourteenth century, when several bright scholars suddenly remembered that Rome had once had a mighty empire that built roads, villas and aqueducts and brought prosperity and progress throughout the Western world. 'Hang on,' thought the bright scholars. 'Why don't we just nick all their ideas?' This triggered a surge of interest in Greek and Roman literature, and became known as humanism on account of one or two of the ancient Romans having being vaguely human. Humanists tried to collect together as much classical knowledge as possible, because it was a lot easier than having to come up with it themselves. They taught it in universities in a course called humanities, which was popular with students as it seemed an easier option than science. They celebrated the advent of the Renaissance man, who was expected to know a dangerously small amount about a lot of different things and also wear nice perfume. Chief among them was Leonardo da Vinci: painter, sculptor, writer, architect, musician, engineer, anatomist and inventor. As well as building a canal, painting *The Last Supper*, and inventing a tank, he was also an expert on human anatomy, a fact scholars say may explain the mysterious smile on the face of the Mona Lisa.

Most of the early Renaissance men were Florentines like Michelangelo, Donatello and Roberto Baggio. But by 1500 the word had spread to northern Europe, aided by the invention of the printing press. The Dutch monk Erasmus wrote books criticising the Church for its corruption and lack of piety. His friend Sir Thomas More penned the famous *Utopia*, in which he imagined a land with no possessions, with no need for greed or hunger, a brotherhood of man, sharing all the world. People said he was a dreamer, but he wasn't the only one. Shakespeare joined in with a few plays, while Flemish painters experimented with oils on canvas. Suddenly Europe was hip, and established ideas were under threat.

The Reformation

MARTIN LUTHER

One of these established ideas was that if, as a good and devout Christian, you wanted to go to heaven after you died, it was important at certain times of the day, if not constantly, to give the Church some money. As God's official agent on Earth, this was the only way the Church could guarantee proper service from their client, for otherwise He would simply take His business to another team who were willing to pay the proper market rate. One way of donating money to the Church was to buy from it an original and wholly authentic holy relic, such as a fragment of the true Holy Cross, which was available in an unlimited supply from the club shop as well as reputable internet sites.

Martin Luther, a black German baptist monk from Alabama, had always felt uneasy about the religious precepts the Church had taught him to follow. But no matter what he did he couldn't quite put his finger on the problem. However, one day when he was reading the Bible, he had a revelation. It was in Latin! That was why he was having trouble understanding it. From that day, he realised that all the fancy stuff the Church was telling him to do was nonsense. All he needed was blind faith.

Luther posted ninety-five theses on the church door at Wittenberg, in which he argued that bishops, priests and popes were an unnecessary distraction from the truth contained in the Bible. Needless to say, this did not go down all that well with bishops, priests and popes, and the following year Luther was forced to submit to a Diet of Worms, in the hope that he would recant his breakfast.

But Luther had a strong constitution. In 1522, he translated the New Testament into German so that he could read it at last, and began to work on the rest. In the meantime, many German rulers took up his cause, attracted by the simplicity of the doctrine and the fact that they could really piss off the Holy Roman Emperor.* New sects of Lutheranism sprung up, like the Anabaptists, and though Luther himself opposed them (he was sure his Latin Bible had said something about no sects before marriage), many others jumped on their bandwagon. When the emperor attempted to stem the tide in 1529 by banning all new religions, the lords protested, giving them the moniker Protestants.

THE REFORMATION SPREADS INTO HENRY VIII

From Germany, Lutheranism quickly spread northwards into Scandinavia, becoming the established church in Denmark, Norway and Sweden. In England, it met opposition in the portly shape of Henry VIII, who felt the only person in his kingdom who needed more sects was himself. This earned him the title Defender of the Faith from the Pope. But a few years later this started to look a bit silly as he attempted to divorce his first wife, Catherine, for giving birth to a foul deformed monstrosity abominated by God and humankind alike.†
The Pope refused to grant the divorce on the entirely

* A popular pastime in Germany at the time, along with witch-burning.

† A girl.

spiritual grounds that Catherine was the aunt of the Holy Roman Emperor, and Henry decided that, rather than beg, he would simply form his own Church. This was basically the same as the Catholic Church, except that Henry was the head of it, and thus had the right not only to divorce his wives but to chop their heads off as well. He also granted himself the power to dissolve monasteries, though he was careful to use acid that was non-corrosive to gold.

He was finally given a son by his third wife, the actress Jane Seymour. Jane died soon after giving birth, which greatly upset Henry as he hadn't even had the chance to execute her. Three more wives followed, but by this time Henry was so nauseously gout-ridden and obese, they were practically executing themselves. His only son, Edward VI, eventually took the throne upon Henry's death in 1547. But he lasted just six years before dying of consumption. This left Henry's first daughter,

FACT

FICTION

QUEEN ELIZABETH 1 - BEFORE AND AFTER PHOTOSHOP.

Mary, to take charge. Bloody Mary's reign was a veritable vodka and tomato of revolts and persecutions, as she attempted to restore Catholicism and burn anyone who remained an Anglican. Thus, no one was upset when she died and was succeeded by the more moderate Elizabeth I, daughter of Anne Boleyn, Henry's second wife and real sexpot. Elizabeth brought peace and prosperity to the realm, but chose not to take a husband for the sake of England's security. At least that's what she liked to tell herself when she saw her hooked nose and black rotting teeth reflected in the mirror.

CALVIN AND THE CALVINISTS

Meanwhile, in the small town of Switzerland, a man named John Calvin had appeared. Calvin was convinced that as far as religious reformation went, Luther had been a bit of a pussy, and believed that not only was faith more important than good works, but that God had in fact already decided who was going to heaven on Judgment Day and there was pretty much nothing we could do about it. Those elected by God had a duty to live up to their position by constantly begging forgiveness for their sins and trying not to look too smug. Of course, nobody could actually know whether they had been elected or not. But Calvin made it clear that if you weren't a Calvinist you could be pretty sure you hadn't been. In 1541, he was invited to take over the city of Geneva and put his beliefs into practice. Genevans were thenceforth prohibited from dancing, smiling, gambling,

CALVIN AND THE CALVINISTS: DANCING, SMILING, GAMBLING, PLAYING CARDS, WEARING NICE CLOTHES AND YODELLING – ALL MADE ILLEGAL.

playing cards, wearing nice clothes, going to the theatre, or – mercifully – yodelling. They could, however, listen quietly to sermons and beat their children to a pulp, and so they did that a lot.

Remarkably, this barmy set of rules caught on, and by 1600 had produced the predominant Protestant Church of Europe. In the northern Netherlands, it became known as the Dutch Reformed Church; in Scotland it was the Presbyterian Church; and in England the Puritan movement. It even reached staunchly Catholic France, in the form of the Huguenots. Clearly, somebody needed to stop it before it was too late. Unfortunately, the

Catholic Church was busy with other things, owing to the unexpected outbreak of . . .

THE WITCH CRAZE

With its institutions under threat, its central doctrines in question and its number of popes slashed to single digits, the Church decided to hit back by holding a series of action-packed, fun-for-all-the-family bonfire nights. The Inquisition was brought over from Spain to organise them and they immediately began scouring Europe for firewood. Unfortunately, with a mini ice age going on, all the firewood had already been used up by peasants, and so the Inquisition was forced to use heretics instead. Heretics burned quite well, but eventually supplies began to run low, pushing the Inquisition to seek elsewhere for its kindling. It was at this point they discovered, almost by chance, a disturbing new phenomenon sweeping through the dark superstitious villages of Europe: old ladies.

Stunned by its previous ignorance of such demonic creatures, the Inquisition swung into action. At first the zealous inquisitors found it hard to determine the truth of the accusations. But eventually they realised that if the defendant truly was an old lady, there was a good chance she would give herself away by drowning when dunked in water. Also she would probably be fond of knitting. Both of these pieces of evidence turned out to be correct, and thus, condemned by their own vile behaviour, old ladies were exposed for what they really were.

The witch craze claimed the lives of tens of thousands of people, particularly in Germany where everybody had always been a bit crazy anyway. It petered out towards the end of the seventeenth century, as the Age of Reason kicked in, but doubts still remain in England as to how Thora Hird managed to live to the age of two hundred and eighty-four.

Test Yourself on the Renaissance and the Reformation
∾

1. If Calvin founded the Calvinists and Luther founded the Lutherans, who founded the Bay City Rollers? And why?

2. When was the last time you enjoyed a really good renaissance? Do you find it happens less often now you're older?

PART II

COUNTRIES TAKE IT IN TURNS TO BE TOP DOG

AD 1500-1750

∾

The Golden Age of Spain

In 1516, King Ferdinand of Spain died, handing over the reins of power to his grandson Charles. Charles was an Austrian Hapsburg born and raised in Flanders, but through a horrible quirk of aristocratic interbreeding he was somehow able to make himself both Charles I of Spain and Charles V of the Holy Roman Empire at the very same time. Nobody could quite understand how he had pulled it off, nor, more to the point, what he had done with Charles II, III and IV. But it gave him an empire that included Spain, Austria, southern Italy, the New World and his Nether regions. Ruling this huge expanse, however, was not easy. Despite his convincing moustache, the Spanish never really accepted him as a Spaniard and kept calling him Charles V to irritate him.

At the same time, the French called him Charles I and insisted that this meant southern Italy and his Nether regions belonged to them, causing constant warfare, now perilously conducted with muskets and cannons.

By 1556, the poor king was exhausted and promptly retired to a monastery, where the monks called him Charles III for a joke. His final words are reported to have been: 'Si quel est un Golden Age, entonces yo es el rey de Sweden.'* His Spanish had always been rudimentary at best. His sensible deathbed order was to divide the empire in two, with the Spanish and Dutch part going to his son Philip II, and the Holy Roman Empire to his brother Ferdinand. This in turn caused confusion, because Ferdinand seemed much more of a Spanish kind of name than Philip, and people wondered if he'd got them the wrong way round. But Philip soon put this straight by starting up the Inquisition again, which was very much a Spanish thing to do.

Philip was big on Catholicism, and spent most of his reign trying to persuade the rest of Europe to be big on Catholicism too, generally by tying them to stakes and setting fire to their legs. He married Bloody Mary to get her to kill off the Protestants in England, and when she died he proposed to her sister Elizabeth so she could carry on the good work. When Elizabeth refused, romantic that he was, the king attempted to woo her with the Spanish Armada.

This, of course, became the scene of one of England's finest historical anecdotes, involving the effeminate

* 'If this is a Golden Age, then I'm the king of Sweden.'

adventurer Sir Francis Drake. When 130 Spanish ships were sighted off the coast of Plymouth, the lackadaisical Drake was still at home fiddling with his bowls. Upon being warned of the grave danger facing England, he is said to have remarked wittily: 'Ah, fighting the Spanish may be hard, but armada,' delaying the navy's response for several hours while they tried to work out what he meant. Eventually, the English fleet set off in pursuit up the Channel, dealt decisively with the dastardly Spanish and created a Protestant wind to blow them into the Irish sea. Many ships went down, and the Spanish were forced to return home, while England felt confident she would rule the waves from then on.

The Golden Age of France

As Spain declined, France rose, and, to the dismay of all, became the top nation of Europe. In 1661, twenty-two-year-old Louis XIV ascended to the throne. Louis was a believer in absolute monarchy, as encapsulated in his famous quote: 'L'état, c'est moi.' *

He kept a lavish court at his new palace at Versailles. In order to maintain his grip on the country, he forced the most important nobles to live with him in the palace. These nobles, as befitting their intellect and status, devoted their time to the discussion of vital state questions, such as: Do I look good in this ruffled silk petticoat and lace cravat? What about these ermine-lined velvet breeches with petite-oie ribbon galants?

* 'Don't eat that, it's mine.'

Ooh, wait, is it time for tea yet? What type of petit biscuit shall we be served today, I wonder? The last question, of course, was a trick one, as the answer was always Bourbon. The real work was done by Louis and his clever bourgeois ministers, like Jean-Baptiste Colbert and François Michel Louvois.

Colbert, the finance minister, was a mercantilist who encouraged the growth of domestic manufacturing at the expense of foreign imports. He imposed heavy tariffs on foreign goods, and when that failed just let the French farmers burn English lorries. In this way, France became the richest country in Europe. Louvois' responsibility was the military, and he too did a fine job. With the famously strict disciplinarian General Martinet in charge, the pair moulded France's ragtag army into a huge, elite force that could sometimes go through an entire day without running away. By the early 1700s, they had 400,000 troops, the largest and most powerful force Europe had ever seen.

The reason they needed so many soldiers was, of course, because Louis kept getting them killed in bloody European free-for-alls, like the War of the Spanish Succession in 1701. This was caused when Charles II of Spain died childless, leaving, by yet another horribly inadvertent act of interbreeding, Louis XIV's grandson as heir. Faced with the prospect of having Bourbons in charge of both France and Spain, the rest of Europe understandably declared war, the final result being that the Bourbons were permitted to take over the Spanish

> He imposed heavy tariffs on foreign goods, and when that failed just let the French farmers burn English lorries.

throne, but with the proviso that the French Bourbon and the Spanish Bourbon could never be the same Bourbon at any particular time. Since nobody could really understand what this meant, the war ended.

By 1713, France was exhausted and broke, but she was still *numéro un*. Though she was often too busy fighting to notice, she had just been through a Golden Age, with various witty playwrights and artists who are probably very famous in France. The rest of Europe slavishly copied her language, etiquette, fashion and food, while all the time protesting how much they hated the country's guts. *Plus ça change*, as the French might say.

The Golden Age of Oliver Cromwell's Warts

THE ENGLISH CIVIL WAR

The Puritans, taking their cue from their founder, John Calvin, were a happy-go-lucky bunch of mild churchgoers, whose only wish was to be allowed to live in peace in order to pursue their hobbies of silent prayer, quiet meditation and monarchal beheading. Some of them had already left for America to do just that, only to find to their chagrin that the first king they wished to behead had stayed behind in England. This king was Charles I, an absolute monarch of a ruler who kept getting people to lend him money even though he had no intention of paying them back, ever.* Charles needed

* Nowadays, of course, this would have earned him a very nice bonus at the Royal Bank of Scotland.

this money in order to fuel a massive and uncontrollable wig habit.

The forced loans allowed the king to rule without the inconvenience of calling parliament. Eventually, however, having secured loans from everybody in the entire country, including Roger his pet hamster, he ran out of money. Compelled at last to undissolve parliament, he then proceeded to demand that they buy him a wig so large and unwieldy it would require the construction of an entire new palace wing. For the parliamentarians, this was too much and, having waited so long to sit, they did not stand up again for the next two years. The Puritans, displaying the kind of creativity and imagination they were renowned for, called it the Long Parliament.

The Long Parliament said they would only lend Charles the money if he accepted certain conditions, such as the execution of his heavy-handed archbishop, William Laud. At first, Charles didn't object to this, as there was a chance he might be able to catch the archbishop's headpiece on the way to the basket. But a few days later, he changed his mind and declared a civil war.

The royal army was nicknamed the Cavaliers, on account of their comical inability to win any serious battles, while the parliamentarians were called Roundheads, in celebration of, quite frankly, who knows what. The first few battles of the war were inconclusive, but in 1643 the two sides met at Marston Moor, where

CROMWELL'S NEW MODEL ARMY –
THE SOLDIERS COULD FLOAT IN THE BATH.

the leader of the parliamentarians, Oliver Cromwell, led a cavalry charge that swept through the royal flanks. Charles ran away, and York fell to the Puritans. A year later, Cromwell formed the New Model Army, in which he removed all the amateur politician commanders and replaced them with professional plastic soldiers, thus allowing his army to float in the bath. This helped him to win the final major battle at Naseby, when, in a bold change of strategy, he led a cavalry charge that swept through the royal flanks.

Charles was captured and taken to Hampton Court, from which he soon made a dramatic escape by walking out through the front door disguised as himself.* Meanwhile, parliament was in a state of uproar* about whether to execute him or not, with the Levellers,

* Plus ça change,
encore une fois.

Diggers, Snoggers and Shaggers saying they should and the Piggers, Doggers, Rockers and Dockers arguing for compromise. In 1648, however, the king made the fatal mistake of allying himself with the Scots and invading the north of England. This gave the Snoggers and Shaggers just the excuse they needed and, having chopped parliament up until only the Rump remained, voted 26 to 20 (with 24 abstentions due to cramp) to execute him. And so it was that on 30 January 1649, before a silent crowd in Whitehall, Charles finally lost his head. This is widely regarded as marking the end of his reign.

BRITAIN BECOMES A DEMOCRACY (KIND OF)

From 1649 to 1660, England had no king and called itself the Commonwealth, thanks to all the wealth being concentrated in the hands of a few landed nobles. Cromwell announced that, to make up for the religiously intolerant years of Charles and Archbishop Laud, people would now be free to worship in any way they wished, so long as it was the Puritan way. Pubs were closed and people were banned from having sexual intercourse, except with farmyard animals. Although this made the Welsh happy, it provoked the Scots and Irish into rebellion, and Cromwell was forced to lead so many cavalry charges it looked as if the Commonwealth might run out of flanks altogether.

When Cromwell died, England quickly went back to having kings again, which brought about the unfortunate succession to the throne of James II, who was, of all things, a Catholic. This was not an ideal quality for a king of England and, in a state of uproar, parliament promptly divided, amoeba-like, into two political parties, the flamboyant, aristocratic Tories and the prudish, puritanical Whigs. The Whigs began passing frantic acts trying to bar Catholics from coming to the throne, while the Tories hit back with yet more frantic acts trying to bar Whigs from coming to their parties. In 1688, in absolute uproar, parliament invited James's daughter Mary and her husband William of Orange to pop over from Holland to take over. Having quickly disposed of their father, William and Mary took the throne, pleasing everyone by agreeing that they were not ruling through divine right but through the right of the MPs who had invited them over. They were very tolerant of everybody and everything, which came as no surprise to the MPs, several of whom had once visited Amsterdam at night.

When William died heirless, Mary's sister Anne took the throne. Anne was the fifty-second monarch of England, which by an incredible coincidence is the same number of weeks as there are in a year. This was quite enough excitement for Anne, who spent the rest of her reign taking a well-deserved break. None of her children survived beyond the age of eleven, and so the Whigs chose the next king on the basis of who happened to be in when they telephoned. Since England and Scotland had now been officially unified by the Act of Union in 1707 – a momentous act that had been welcomed by everyone* – they decided it would probably be diplomatic to be ruled by a German.

Thus was born the reign of King George I of Hanover. George made it his policy to spend most of his time outside England, but far from being in uproar, parliament realised this was quite a good thing as it allowed the rise of Sir Robert Walpole, who moved into 10 Downing Street and thus became the first Prime Minister. Walpole was a Whig MP and spent most of his time in power trying to make sure the Tories never got inside his cabinet. He achieved this eventually by labelling them all 'Jacobites', which, as far as anyone could make out, was a kind of prehistoric fish. The fact there was no evidence for it did not matter. Walpole had shown that unsubstantiated name-calling was the way to win elections, and in this way can be credited with the founding of modern parliamentary democracy.

*Except the Scots and the English.

Test Yourself on Top Dog in Europe

1. What happened to the Whigs anyway? You don't see them around much.

2. Discuss the consequences of interbreeding in European aristocratic families, with particular reference to Prince Charles's ears.

PART III

EUROPE DISCOVERS THE WORLD

AD 1492–1763

๑๏

The Age of Exploration

To Europeans in the fifteenth century, the world looked something like this:

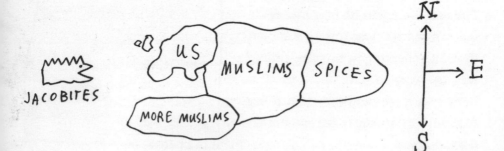

For centuries, medieval European explorers had dreamed of finding a way to reach the mysterious East, without having to launch a crusade to get there.

Unfortunately, every time they thought they had found a way, they woke up with spit dribbling from their mouths and had to start thinking all over again.

But in the fifteenth century, Europe was rocked by the chance discovery that wood, when placed in water, tended to float. At the same time, merchants returning from the Orient had brought back magnetic compasses, which canny European scholars noticed were marked with symbols for both East and West. Suddenly, the whole concept of 'left' now made sense and a new horizon beckoned.

Things got off the ground with the birth of Henry the Navigator. Henry, using his innate navigational skills, managed to find his way to the mythical land of Portugal, where he opened up a school for other people with unusual names, like Amerigo Vespucci and Vasco da Gama. Vasco da Gama rounded the Cape of Good Hope in 1497 and thereby opened up his passage to Indians. He came back laden with spices, for this was what the East was found to be made of, and Europe, heavily pregnant, was seized by a sudden craving for nutmeg.

In Italy, meanwhile, Christopher Columbus had heard from a fella down the pub that the Earth was not, as everyone had previously imagined, made of cheese, but was in fact round, like an Edam. Columbus accepted the support of the Spanish and set off with three ships and a compass to take advantage of the earth's newfound circularity to get to India. Seventy-three days, two mutinies and several bouts of scurvy later, he reached the Bahamas, which were nowhere near India but try telling that to a man who's been living on his own urine for the past two months. He found the natives there friendly, if slightly confused, and promptly claimed the islands for Spain.

Then, in 1519, Magellan set off on a record round-the-world voyage, crossing the Atlantic, rounding Cape Horn, entering the South Sea (which he renamed the Pacific, on account of its placidness), getting smashed to bits amidst the Pacific's routine fifty-foot waves, eating rats to survive, starving to death, eating sawdust to survive, starving again, eating his first lieutenant to survive, starving once more, eating most of his ship to survive, before finally arriving with relief and triumph at the Philippines, where he was promptly beaten to death by the natives. Only one of the original five ships survived the voyage. But eventually its captain, Sebastián del Cano, made it back to Europe, thereby proving to the world once and for all that it was time Europe started building better boats.

Empire Hunting

Soon exploring the world wasn't enough for Europe's great maritime nations. In a historic joint venture, Spain and Portugal decided to conquer then destroy it as well. To make this task more interesting, however, they created a rule whereby no conquest could be attempted with an army any larger than, say, a basketball team. Hernando Cortés* took the lead in 1519 by taking on the mighty Aztec Empire aided by three companions and a horse, kind of like *Monkey Magic*. However, he was soon outdone by his compatriot Pizarro, who managed to conquer the all-powerful Incas with the help only of a clockwork mouse and his dog Jack. From these bases in Mexico and Peru, the Spanish moved into both North and South America, colonising, converting and enslaving wherever they went.

* See p.109

Disease and maltreatment soon put paid to the local Indians – the Mexican population, for example, fell from 10 million in 1519 to just 1.5 million a century later, all achieved without the aid of human sacrifice. But when they ran out of Indians, the Spanish realised they could simply import black slaves from Africa, delivered in convenient boat-sized packages across the Atlantic. The people in charge of this lucrative trade in the sixteenth century were the Portuguese, who, as part of their agreement with the Spanish, had concentrated their genocide in Africa and India. With trading posts spread all over the Pacific from Macao to Timbuktu, they filled their boats to the brim with spices from Asia and slaves from West Africa. There was competition, of course, from Arab traders, but the Portuguese sailed with cannons, which they would throw at the Arabs if they got too close. Still, the heavily laden ships often sank in the stormy ocean waters, sometimes – tragically – with spices on board.

❝ Hernando Cortés took the lead in 1519 by taking on the mighty Aztec empire aided by three companions and a horse, kind of like *Monkey Magic*. ❞

The Dutch, French and English, meanwhile, watched the way Spanish explorers had travelled the globe, sowing death, disease and destruction wherever they went, and thought: 'That looks like fun.' The Netherlands, under the guise of their evil multinational Dutch East India Company, took over much of the Pacific spice trade and set up a colony in South Africa. The French plumped for Canada, which they bumped into accidentally on the way to the Northwest Passage. The Canadian settlement grew slowly, owing to the difficulty people had with locating Canada on a map. However, by the mid-eighteenth century it had as many as 60,000 inhabitants.*

* Just a few more than Canada's population today.

This left the English. Their first real experience of America came in 1607, when James I granted the London Company a charter to establish a permanent colony at Jamestown in Virginia. Unbeknownst to the London Company, however, this was one of James I's infamous 'joke-charters' because – get this – there was no town called James in Virginia! Consequently, most of their employees starved to death trying to find it. The next settlers were, of course, the Puritans in 1620. They had more luck, owing to the helpfulness of local Native Americans, who gave them a turkey and thus taught them the true meaning of Christmas. Although life was harsh, they were able to generate warmth in the long, cold winters by setting fire to suspected witches.

Eventually, more people came, and by 1732 there were thirteen colonies strewn along the east coast. They attracted misfits from all across Europe – Jews, Germans, Irish, Italians, Piers Morgan – all living together in large melting-pots. Since many were poor and illiterate, they were forced to invent a crude, primitive language in order to communicate with each other. This became known as American English. The colonists grew tobacco and cotton for export back home. For this, of course, they needed workers, and, after a brief and unsatisfactory experiment with doing it themselves, quickly opted for African slaves.

Britain Becomes Top Dog

Empire-building proved to be a massively profitable exercise. So much gold was being brought into Europe that it was now even more plentiful than rats and dung, causing a dramatic change in people's diets. Profits soared, and rich men rushed to invest in the ruthless corporations that were given a monopoly over trade. National banks sprang up, as did the first stock exchange in Amsterdam. Lloyd's of London even started selling insurance in the unlikely event of trade being disrupted by war, fire etc.

This heralded a period of international wars, conducted, as usual, with fire. These wars had two rules:

1. They were to be so confusing that nobody ever had any idea whose side they were on.

2. Except Britain, who always won.

In 1701, the War of the Spanish Succession broke out in Europe, while, in America, Queen Anne's War began at about the same time. For eleven years wars were fought on both continents simultaneously, with nobody quite understanding why or what was going on. It was not until 1713, when the War of the Spanish Succession ended and hostilities in America mysteriously ceased too, that people realised the answer: they were both the same war! Everybody then had a good chuckle about it, especially Britain, who, needless to say, had won.

In 1739, Britain and Spain fought the War of Jenkins' Ear, after an English merchant captain had his ear cut off by the Spanish costguard. It was a conflict that nobody believed could really be happening until Captain Jenkins actually showed everyone his severed ear and revealed that, sure enough, there was a war taking place there. It was eventually settled in nobody's favour with antibiotics. Then came the War of the Austrian Succession, called King George's War in American English; and after that in 1756 the French and Indian War or Seven Years War. This was the most confusing of the lot, because it sounded like the French were fighting against the Indians when in fact they were both on the same side. But if that was the case, who *were* they fighting against? Was Britain involved? If not, how on earth was she supposed to win? Moreover, were the Indians actually Indians? Weren't they Native Americans? If so, what were they doing in India?

These were questions that plagued Europe in the eighteenth century. In 1763, everybody was so cranky and exhausted they signed the Treaty of Paris so that they could finally get a bit of peace and quiet. Despite some late confusion during the long summit, when tired negotiators attempted to award France to the Indians, the treaty confirmed Britain's wartime gains. She had taken all of France's possessions in North America, and now shared the continent with ailing Spain. She also got France's outposts in Africa, and took control of the trade in India. This gave her the world's largest colonial empire, and marked her arrival as Europe's official Top Dog. Hurrah.

Test Yourself on the Age of Discovery

1. Complete the following well-known mnemonic:

**In fourteen hundred and ninety-two
Columbus sailed the ocean blue.
In fifteen hundred and twenty-two
Cannibals ate Magellan's ....**

2. Counter-factual history: how would the world today be different if it actually had turned out to be flat? Discuss with special reference to Richard Branson and hot-air ballooning.

7.

REVOLUTION, BABY
(AD 1700-1815)

Introduction

As Europe stormed its way into the Early Modern Period, it was feeling pretty good about itself. In the last couple of centuries, it had had a renaissance: it had conquered the world, invented capitalism and secured enough spices to cater for several generations of post-beer Indian takeaway customers. Best of all for Europe, it was now dominated by Britain. But, as ever, change was on its way. More than change, in fact. Revolutions. An American Revolution, a French Revolution, an Industrial Revolution, even a Scientific Revolution. By 1815, the world would be a far different place: enlightened by reason, delighted by treason, and drowning in smog.

PART I

THE AGE OF REASON

AD 1700-1800

⌁

The Scientific Revolution

To people in the Middle Ages, there were certain immutable and undeniable truths about the world in which they lived:

1) It was flat.

2) It was at the centre of the universe.

3) It had taken six days to build.

4) It was a bit shit.

This was not a time when people thought a great deal about reason and logic. Everything that existed on Earth, no matter how pointless, was part of God's grand design, up to and including phlegm. Nowadays we know that phlegm is simply the secretion of mucus by the respiratory tract; to the medieval mind, however, it seemed to offer direct, unequivocal proof of the divine origins of the Welsh language.

Clearly, the world was in need of some serious updating, and from the sixteenth century a number of brave Europeans set about doing this. Magellan, of course, had put paid to the first truth by proving that urine could be drunk in equally great quantities in both the northern and southern hemispheres. The second one, however, took longer to crack, owing to the Church's long-standing custom of setting fire to anyone who disagreed with it. Copernicus was the first to mention its potential fallacy, but his claims were not taken seriously as he was a monk and, as such, not entitled to wear an outlandishly large and ridiculous wig. Brahe and Kepler then provided more evidence through astronomical observation, but it wasn't until Galileo was persecuted by the Church in 1632 for spreading vile heretical lies that people began to realise it must be true.

Sir Isaac Newton finally settled the argument later in the century by devising a series of laws that regulated how planets were to move from now on. They were called Newton's Three Laws of Motion, and they created quite a stir in the solar system at first, as the penalty for breaking them involved crashing into the sun. Briefly put, they stated that: (1) All planets must remain in their present state of motion, except in an emergency; (2) Every action must have a reaction, so if, for example, one planet cut across another planet's orbit without signalling, the second planet had the right to get out of its vehicle and punch the first planet in the tropics; (3) No parking in Uranus.

Newton became the pin-up model of the new wave of scientists, heading up the Royal Society in London

NEWTON'S THIRD LAW OF MOTION:
NO PARKING ON URANUS.

and publishing work on everything from mathematics to alchemy. He died in 1727 at the age of two hundred and forty-eight, tragically crushed to death by a falling apple. His laws, however, lived on, and are still obeyed today by most major planets, except near Black Holes.

The Enlightenment

While scientists were making up laws to govern the universe, French philosophers were working on their own theories of how to drink as much red wine as possible without anybody noticing they hadn't paid for it. This was known as the Enlightenment, and it ushered in an age of democracy, egalitarianism and free-drinking.

The two most significant figures of the Enlightenment were Voltaire, inventor of the battery, and Jean-Jacques Rousseau, the underwater film-maker. Voltaire became the spokesperson of the movement with his crusade against injustice, tyranny and corruption. This often led to run-ins with Louis XV, because, by an astonishing coincidence, injustice, tyranny and corruption were the very three things the king had been planning to base his government on. The writer kept getting banged up in the Bastille, and then, the moment he was released, announcing his freedom with words like, 'In general, the art of government consists in taking as much money as possible from one class of citizens to give to the other', whereupon he would immediately be thrown into the Bastille again.

His contemporary Rousseau generally avoided prison, but he made up for it by being obnoxious, paranoid and sexually deviant. Of course, just because he was paranoid did not mean everybody did not hate him, because they did; and they liked it when he got himself whipped by his schoolmaster's sister. But other than that, Rousseau was a great thinker, who believed in the nobility of the savage and who spread the idea that government should be based upon popular sovereignty. He came up with the catchphrase 'liberté, égalité, fraternité'* and once said, 'Man is born free and everywhere he is in chains', a state he liked to find himself in whenever possible.

* 'Soft, strong, and very long.'

Enlightened Despots: Prussians and Austrians

Prussia was one of those states that nobody took very seriously until it suddenly became too big to control, rather like Simon Cowell's ego. It achieved this in true

Germanic style by participating in every major war it could find and, if it couldn't find any, by starting one itself. The man most responsible for this was Frederick the Great, who came to the throne in 1740. Frederick made it his ambition to make war with every race of people in the entire world, including the Austrians, the French, the Polish, the Russians, the Swedish and even, at one point, the ancient Assyrians.

Strangely, this had not seemed a likely course during Frederick's early years. As a child, he had been more interested in reading philosophy, playing the flute and writing poetry than leading macho Prussian armies. It got to the point where his father was even beginning to suspect his son might be enlightened. At first, he tried to reason Frederick out of his condition, and when that failed just put him in prison instead. This did the trick, and from that point Frederick became just as unpredictably aggressive as the next German. But it did not entirely cure him of his enlightenment, however. Frederick spent much of his reign tolerating religions, improving education, patronising the arts and banning judicial torture. The latter, of course, quickly became a major headache for the Prussian police force, until they realised they could still secure all the false confessions they needed by utilising Frederick's other great passion, German opera.

Frederick shared his enlightened ways with his Hapsburg rival, Joseph II of Austria. Joseph's enlightenment was based on kidnapping musical child prodigies like Mozart, whom the emperor would dress in frilly clothing and force to perform vigorous piano concertos in front of court audiences. This, of course, drove his neighbour Frederick insane with jealousy, and the result was twenty-three years of almost constant warfare between the two. Frederick eventually won these wars, only to find to his despair that Mozart had grown up by then and started school. Instead he had to be content with stealing the rich province of Silesia, which he added to Prussia's burgeoning territory.

Enlightened Despots: Russians

Russia, meanwhile, was still having history of its own, even though it wasn't something people paid a lot of attention to. In 1682, however, a new czar by the name of Peter the Great came to the throne, and immediately began to set Russia on a new path. He was only ten years old, but he was smarter than all the other boys in his class* and, at six foot seven inches tall, able to see further than any Russian ruler in history. His view, in fact, extended all the way into Western Europe, and he paid a visit early on to try to unlock its secrets. He even went as far as working as a carpenter in Holland in order to learn the art of shipbuilding, until he was caught trying to take his work home with him.

Back in the motherland, he set about modernising his country. He began with small things, like revolutionising Russia's education system, its administrative institutions,

* At least, he always seemed to get the best marks.

and antiquated agricultural structure, and then moved on to far more essential matters: getting men to shave off their beards and forcing women to wear shorter skirts, so that they'd look more like those girls he'd seen in the windows in Amsterdam. Then he had a go at the army. The Russian army at this time was not taken very seriously by the West, due to the fact that its major military tactic consisted of luring the enemy into vast, windswept plains and waiting for them to slowly freeze to death in the snow. Peter, however, was determined to show that the Russians were really just one P short of being Prussians. He enlarged the force, reorganised them and built a navy. Then, just for something to do, he declared war on Sweden.

After Peter's death in 1725, Russia had a few worthless rulers for a while, until the German princess Catherine the Great was able to subtly manoeuvre herself on to the throne by murdering her husband. Like Frederick and Joseph, Catherine considered herself to be an enlightened despot, in the sense that she sometimes listened to classical music in the bath. She also made her nobles speak French, a language that their starving servants, of course, could not understand. This was probably a good thing, as the nobles tended to say things like, 'Ivan, old friend, what do you fancy having for dinner tonight, oven-roasted peasant or deep-fried serf?' within earshot. Eventually, however, this led to a huge peasant uprising, which Catherine, genuinely upset that her subjects could be so unhappy with her enlightened rule, brutally crushed with the army.*

So, what made Catherine great? Put it this way, it wasn't her vegetarian lasagna. Rather, it was war on the Ottoman Turks, who were by now comfortably settling into their role as the sick men of Europe. She beat them in short order, and was only prevented from wiping them out completely by pleas from other European leaders, who were afraid they wouldn't be able to afford the medical bills. Russia gained some ports on the Black Sea, a protectorate of Crimea and a free pass through Ottoman territory to the Mediterranean coast, which was excellent for holidays.

* In French.

Test Yourself on the Age of Reason
ω

1. The Age of Reason. Why?

PART II

THE AGE OF REVOLUTION

AD 1763-1815

The American Revolution

Why are Americans always revolting? That was the question on Britain's lips as she entered the fateful year that would become known the world over as 1763. She really couldn't understand it. She had the best system of government in the world, with her cool constitutional monarchy and nowadays only occasional beheading of spouses, and all she demanded from her colonies in return was blind obedience to Britain's insane, babbling king and all their money. What was wrong with these people? The Americans, however, felt that paying taxes to a country that was not only three thousand miles away but also had a totally different spelling system was not common sense, and so when Britain tried to impose a new tax called the Stamp Tax to pay for the French and

A LESS BORING HISTORY OF THE WORLD

Indian War,* the Americans, as they had been taught to do from childhood, attempted to sue them.

The British quickly caved in, because, although the thirteen colonies had a combined population of just one and a half million, almost 90 per cent of them were lawyers. Under the encouragement of the wily, incoherent George III, they attempted to diffuse the tension by abolishing the unpopular old Stamp Tax and replacing it with a new exactly-the-same tax, which they called the Townshend Tax, for no other reason than it alliterated. Unfortunately, the colonists saw through this ingenious ploy, and were so furious they dumped tea into Boston harbour. The British were outraged, as the uncouth Americans had poured the milk in first and hadn't even bothered to warm the pot, and, in an absolute uproar, parliament passed the Intolerable Acts, which, among other things, made it illegal for American colonists ever to pass one another on the street without saying 'Have a nice day!' in a loud and annoyingly friendly voice. In the circumstances, war seemed inevitable, particularly when, in spring 1775, British and American troops started shooting at each other.

This was the Battle of Lexington, named after one of its most prominent protagonists, Paul Revere. Nobody was quite sure who had won it, as it took place at night. But the Americans clearly thought they had, because they declared independence shortly afterwards. They did this in an historic document called the Declaration of Independence, penned by Thomas Jefferson, a tall

Virginian slave-owner who believed all men were created equal, except the ones who belonged to him.

The war went on for the next eight years, but the colonists finally won after they discovered a small but fatal flaw in the British strategy: all their soldiers were still in England. They celebrated their newfound freedom by drawing up a constitution, which was founded on the principle of checks and balances, allowing the government to write itself checks without worrying if the budget never balances. This became the inspiration for future democratic governments the world over. A few years later, they added amendments, guaranteeing US citizens certain basic and inalienable rights, such as the freedom to buy fully loaded handguns from vending machines and use them on anyone who threatened to, say, walk past. The British left town quickly, as did the French and the Indians. Suddenly, Mad King George didn't seem so bonkers after all.

The French Revolution

THE CAUSES OF THE FRENCH REVOLUTION

What were the causes of the French Revolution? This is a question that, in a very real sense, was guaranteed to come up on the exam paper, allowing generations of schoolchildren to memorise the answer beforehand. The response they would always give, of course, was the Boston Tea Party. This is because they were sixteen and had other things on their mind.*

* Generally related to Baywatch.

The actual answer had more to do with bread than tea, in that the French king and his nobles ate it whenever they wanted, while the townsfolk and peasants could only have it on certain occasions, such as when it was needed for throwing at poor people in the stocks. There was also the problem of taxation. Under the current system, clergymen and landowners were exempt from paying tax, for the very good reason that they didn't want to. The entire tax burden fell on the members of the so-called Third Estate, which covered everyone from wealthy bourgeoisie to impoverished hunchbacked bell-ringers. This was bad enough when times were plentiful, but in the late 1700s rising food prices, coupled with the spiralling costs of Marie Antoinette's hair, led to growing discontent. To make matters worse, France was broke, and Louis XVI realised that the only way he was going to pay for his wife's latest visit to the coiffeur was to raise taxes. Unfortunately, nobody in the Third Estate had anything left to be taxed, and so Louis regretfully turned to the nobility.

The nobles listened carefully to their king's proposal to tax them, but argued cogently against it on the grounds that they would rather not. This complex legal position persuaded Louis that he needed help, and so he called together a meeting of the Estates-General. The Estates-General was an obscure body that had last met 175 years before, and everybody was very excited at the prospect of its comeback, even though they couldn't quite recall what it was for or who sat on it. The First and Second Estates, representing the clergy and nobility, remembered it as an august body that discussed the most pressing problems of the land and, after careful consideration, voted 2–1 not to do anything about them. The Third Estate, however, felt that this was not fair, considering that they represented about 99 per cent of the population, and pressed for a system of one man one vote. When the king refused to rule on the matter, the Third Estate walked out and held their own assembly at a nearby tennis court. Louis was beside himself with frustration, because the delegates were standing right where he wanted to serve, and he finally had no choice but to accede to their demands.

At the same time, however, he was determined not to let the situation get out of hand, and he hatched a secret plot to call the army up from the provinces. Unfortunately, the army's clandestine march to Paris was given away by the noise of the drums they had to bang in order to keep time, and the capital erupted into turmoil. On 14 July, angry crowds, spotting the opportunity for a national holiday, stormed the Bastille in search of weapons, and the city fell under the revolutionary command of the war hero General Lafayette. The rest of France now underwent a Great Fear, as everybody suddenly became terrified of everybody else. Townspeople attacked clergy, clergy attacked peasants, peasants attacked nobles, nobles attacked serfs, and serfs – never ones to let an opportunity slip by – attacked sheep. The Revolution had begun.

France was broke, and Louis XVI realised that the only way he was going to pay for his wife's latest visit to the coiffeur was to raise taxes.

THE RISE OF THE GUILLOTINE

In the midst of this turmoil, the Estates-General, now dominated by the bourgeoisie, began voting on a new constitution for France. On 27 August, they produced the Declaration of the Rights of Man, which declared that all men were equal right up to the moment they were born. A few days later, a plucky Parisian housewife named Olympe proposed a Declaration of the Rights of Women, which the National Assembly debated carefully in a closed session, before laughing so hard they were almost sick. Finally, they produced a constitution, dividing France up into executive, legislative and judicial branches, each carefully designed to cancel out the work of the other two. The powerful Legislative Assembly was composed of wealthy bourgeoisie who became either conservatives, radicals or moderates, depending on which seats were free in the assembly hall. The Feuillant conservatives took the seats on the right and the Jacobin radicals those on the left, leaving the moderates to hang precariously from the ceiling above.

In 1792, they were goaded into temporary unity by an invasion by Austria and Prussia, who had decided they didn't like the idea of men having rights so close to their borders. In the ensuing panic, Paris fell under the control of a group of radical hippies, who turned it into a commune. They imprisoned the king and forced the Legislative Assembly to start drawing up a new constitution.

The new constitution was based upon the principle of executing anything that strayed too close to the guillotine. They began with the king in 1793, and, after that proved a hit, followed it up with his wife, and then his ministers, his advisers, his courtiers, his dogs, his toys, his oranges, his turnips, anything vaguely circular in fact. Then they got to work on the rest of the population. Egged on by the psychotic Robespierre, the Jacobins spread the word that the Revolution was the cure for all of France's most serious problems, including garlic breath, which in a sense it was.

* By chopping off his head.

The Terror did not end until some of Robespierre's more moderate associates persuaded him to relax his persecution.* This gave the Legislative Assembly time to make several important contributions to European society, such as universal male suffrage, the metric system and the ten-day working week. This immediately provoked war with Great Britain and Spain, who wanted to know what on earth the French were planning to do with Saturday and Sunday. Remarkably, the revolutionary forces won it, spurred on by patriotic fervour and the inability of the invading coalition forces to understand their new metric road signs.

THE FRENCH REVOLUTIONARY CONSTITUTION BASED ON A PRINCIPLE OF CHOPPING THE HEAD OFF ANYTHING THAT STRAYED TOO CLOSE TO THE GUILLOTINE.

THE RISE OF NAPOLEON

In 1795, members of the Legislative Assembly decided to write a new constitution, as the old one had accidentally got red wine spilled on it. This time they did away with universal male suffrage, because, quite frankly, it had been a pain counting all those votes, and restricted the franchise to themselves, a few of their rich mates and a bloke called Pierre they had met in the pub. They then elected five directors who would take charge of the country.

For the next four years, the five directors devoted themselves to the governing of France, sometimes managing to work for stretches of two or even three hours without attempting to murder each other. As the economy collapsed, prices skyrocketed, and corruption reigned, people accused the directors of doing absolutely nothing with the power they had been given. Although this was somewhat unfair, as the five men did occasionally play musical chairs during meetings, the country was soon impoverished, not to mention poor, and it was clear that yet another new constitution was needed.

Fortunately, some of the leaders of the Legislative Assembly had a better idea. They had begun to think that a strong, dictatorial leader with a penchant for invading Europe might be the answer to France's ills. They kept their ear to the ground for a suitable candidate, which was a good job because if they had looked any higher they wouldn't have seen him. Napoleon Bonaparte had stopped growing at the age of seven, and was about the size of a man's hand. He had risen quickly through the ranks of the French army through the cunning tactic of being too small for the guillotine, and had reached the rank, if not the height, of general by the age of twenty-six.

He was thrust into power in 1799 by a *coup d'état*, and for the first and last time in European history the peace of the continent was about to be threatened by a megalomaniac French dwarf.*

* Not including Nicolas Sarkozy.

The Napoleonic Era

Napoleon quickly showed he was not going to abandon the democratic ideals of the Revolution by holding a plebiscite over the new constitution he proposed: people could either vote 'yes' if they wanted Napoleon as a dictator, or 'no' if they preferred to be tortured. Winning a respectable 104 per cent of the vote, the new leader used his mandate to negotiate a truce with the other

NAPOLEON — STOPPED GROWING AT THE AGE OF SEVEN.

European powers, bringing much-needed peace and stability to the region for a period of almost three whole days. In 1804, however, the young Corsican decided to crown himself emperor of France, which immediately set the other rulers on edge, as France didn't actually have an empire. War broke out the following year.

From the outset, the Napoleonic Wars followed a predictable pattern: France attacks, continental Europe surrenders, Britain heroically holds out. In 1805, Napoleon crushed Austrian and Russian forces at Austerlitz, and thenceforth dominated the continent from Spain to Poland. The same year, however, saw the Battle of Trafalgar, in which Admiral Nelson, directing Britain's fleet from the top of a huge column in London, foiled Napoleon's invasion plans by bombarding his ships with pigeon droppings. Although the commander was killed during the battle, when he tried to sneak in a crafty snog with Hardy, his first lieutenant, Trafalgar ensured Britain's mastery of the seas. From then on, the two sides were locked into a stalemate, as Britain concentrated all her forces at sea and France kept hers on land, preventing their soldiers from ever meeting, except on occasional trips to the seaside. Napoleon attempted to starve the nation of shopkeepers into submission by organising a blockade, denying British holidaymakers much-needed supplies of cheap cigarettes and plonk. But the plucky islanders held on.

The situation remained deadlocked until 1812, when Russia got bored and broke the blockade. An irate

Napoleon invaded with 600,000 troops, only to find that the sneaky Russians had all left the country some time ago, leaving behind nothing but scorched earth and a few angry peasants. Reaching Moscow, he discovered to his horror that the capital had been burned down as well, giving him no choice but to lead his forces on an organised retreat back to France,* whereupon they all slowly froze to death on the vast, windswept plains.

The Russians then miraculously reappeared, and, following the footprints Napoleon had left in the snow, joined the rest of Europe in pursuing him to Paris. The capital became so full of people there wasn't even room for its diminutive emperor, and Napoleon was sent off to the Tuscan island resort of Elba with a pension and a gold watch. There he wrote his most famous palindrome, 'Able was I, ere I saw Elba'. A year later, however, he effected a dramatic escape by concealing himself inside his manservant's shirt pocket, and made a triumphant return to Paris. He ruled there for a hundred days, until the Duke of Wellington finally booted him out for good at Waterloo. This time he was exiled to the dismal island of St Helena in the South Atlantic, where he now lives quietly with his wife and two dogs.

* *Lead* in the sense, that is, of *abandon*, since Napoleon was keen to get back to Paris first, where his tea was waiting.

Test Yourself on the Age of Revolution ↜

1. Put the following in order of maximum embarrassment to French people: Waterloo, Agincourt, Trafalgar, the 2010 World Cup.

2. 'Two heads are better than one' (Voltaire). Discuss with reference to the Reign of Terror.

PART III

THE INDUSTRIAL REVOLUTION

AD 1750-1820

⧸⧹

New Inventions

It is important to remember that, unlike the political revolutions that took place in America and France, the Industrial Revolution occurred in the north of England and was chiefly about cloth caps and whippets. In 1700, for example, to create a really good quality cloth cap from scratch required months of hard effort and grind. But by 1800, thanks to the miracle of mass production, a child of seven was able to make an entire batch in one go simply by operating dangerous heavy machinery for sixteen hours a day. Better still, he could do it at almost no cost *and* without requiring breaks!

Of course, such progress did not happen overnight. Indeed, it took many years of sweat and inspiration before miraculous inventions like the spinning jenny, flying shuttle, spitting mule, frolicking loom and crapping nanny were found to be just jokes the wise-cracking northerners had made up to confuse the shandy-drinking poofters from south of Birmingham. By then, however, it was too late, and there were factories and mills everywhere, churning out so many cheap cloth caps even French nobles caught up in the Revolution were tempted into buying them.

As the machines got bigger and the children smaller, more efficient ways to power the factories became necessary. Since water power had its limitations, inventors turned to steam.* James Watt produced the first practical steam engine in 1763, and that in turn led to a demand for coal, which was freely available from pits conveniently located underground. Then they needed a way to transport the coal from A to B, and built canals, tarmacked roads and even railways for the purpose, until some bright spark – possibly Michael Faraday – pointed out that 'from A to B' was just a figure of speech and they didn't actually need connecting. That triggered more frantic building, and in 1829 George Stephenson's *Rocket* managed to pull a line of cars from Liverpool to Manchester in only two hours one minute – just twenty minutes less than the journey takes today.

* Before condensing back into water when they touched cold surfaces.

Dark, Satanic Yorkshire

Of course, such progress had its price, especially in terms of living and working conditions. Many workers were forced to labour in conditions that nowadays would be regarded as fit only for patients in the National Health Service. The following reminiscences of a Yorkshire-born worker are typical:

> It were hell on earth, I tell yer. I mean, we laboured fourteen hour a day surrounded by nowt but filth an' garbage. It were soul-destroying, mind-numbing. Yer ears were bleedin' with all the noise and yer 'ands were so raw you could barely feel 'em. Then you come home at the end of yer shift, so knackered you c'n barely put key in t' door, and yer find there's nowt to put on't table. Not a crumb of food. So you got the kids hollerin' and the missus screamin' and you jus' wonder what the Good Lord put you on't this earth fer. Hell, I tell yer. It were just hell. Anyway, sorry, what was t' question again? What, mill working? Ah, no, sorry, don't know anything about that. I'm a stockbroker. I thought you were talking about the day Waitrose ran out of Delia Smith's oven-baked salmon with spicy parmesan crust.

It would be wrong, however, to think that it was all doom and gloom for people in Britain. The Industrial Revolution gave citizens many things they hadn't had before, such as secure employment, housing, tuberculosis, cholera and cot death. It also fostered a great sense of community and togetherness. Close-knit neighbourhoods grew up in the inner cities close to the factories, places where entire communities could live and sleep together in harmony, often in the same room.

Through this happy-go-lucky spirit, Britain became the envy of the world. Although British workers were poor – and, in many cases, dead – they were proud, and the goods they produced spread quickly around the globe, providing millions of people with minutes and sometimes hours of good use before breaking down and having to be sent back under warranty. The mark 'Made in Britain' served as a guarantee that the product had real and genuine worth, and the descendants of those hard-working industrial pioneers can be proud of the fact that this statement is just as true today as it was way back then.*

* Because of scarcity value.

Test Yourself on the Industrial Revolution

1. Spot the odd one out: Sheffield, Bradford, Birmingham, the French Riviera.

(Hint: only one of these places was the hometown of snooker legend Joe Johnson)

8.

THE WORLD GETS OBSESSED BY ISMS

(AD 1815-1914)

Introduction

The years from 1815 to 1900 were ones of great progress for the West. Men and women like Michael Faraday, Marie Curie, Charles Darwin and Sigmund Freud were transforming the way people viewed the world around them, particularly their mothers. Atomic theory, electricity, X-rays, penicillin, radioactivity, evolution, repressed sexual desire for one's nanny: these were just some of the advances made in the so-called Age of Progress. One of the most neurotic leaders of all time – Napoleon Bonaparte – was gone, and a new European order was growing up in his place. Long repressed feelings of nationalism, socialism, liberalism and imperialism were being released through therapy, and by 1914 Europe would feel uninhibited enough to engage in the longest stretch of Prozac-inspired insanity the world had ever known.

PART I

LIBERALISM IN BRITAIN, FRANCE AND AMERICA

AD 1815–1914

ᕦᕤ

The Balance of Power After Napoleon

After Napoleon had been exiled to St Helena, all the great powers of Europe sat down for a congress in Vienna to work out what the new balance of power was. This was not an easy thing to do as the balance of power kept shifting depending on which side of the table the well-fed Austrian foreign minister was placed. One minute he would be sitting quite comfortably in the middle, and the next he would suddenly get up, causing the whole room to tilt. The foreign minister's name was Prince Metternich, and he cast a giant shadow across Europe for the next thirty years, particularly when the sun was behind him.

Metternich's primary aim was to find a way to stop the European powers invading each other all the time, as it was forever interrupting his lunch. The major stumbling block to achieving this was, of course, France, who, according to official historical records, had not been able to stay within her own borders since the advent of continental drift. The other European powers tried to ensure she did so from now on by surrounding her with small dispensable buffer countries, such as Belgium and Luxembourg. Belgium's role was to slow down the French advance just long enough to allow the Germans to invade from the other side.

Together with his fellow leaders, Metternich established what became known as the Concert of Europe. This involved creating a set of intermeshing alliances so complex and difficult to understand that no nation could ever feel safe to declare war again, just in case they found themselves fighting on the same side as Italy. Thanks to this clever system, Europe somehow managed to remain at peace for a period of almost forty years, a feat not managed again until the second half of the twentieth century.*

* As long as you ignore the conflict in the former Yugoslavia, which of course most people in Europe did.

Liberalism in Britain

Britain at this time was the envy of the world. Nations from as close as continental Europe and as far away as Scotland were looking at her booming industrial economy, her burgeoning trade empire and her stable political system, and thinking, 'Well, at least they can't play football.' However, beneath the surface things were not quite so rosy. The reason British democracy was so stable was because the right to vote was restricted to people who, either through birth or good fortune, happened to be the Earl of Marlborough. There were also problems with some of the MPs sitting in parliament. An inspection of the House in the 1830s revealed that well over a third of the MPs had, in fact, died during the eighteenth century, but nobody had noticed owing to them mainly being Liberal Democrats. These so-called 'rotten' MPs came from boroughs that, because of urban migration and severe water erosion, didn't actually exist any more, and eventually there were calls to remove them from the benches, at least the ones that weren't stuck. This led to a Reform Bill.

The opposition, however, was not silenced. As the 1830s wore on, Britain began to suffer from a rash of Chartism, when millions of otherwise sane individuals suddenly decided that the solution to all of the country's many social and political woes lay in the creation of a Citizens' Charter. The Charter stipulated that all adult males between the ages of eighteen and eighty-one should be allowed to vote in elections by secret ballot if the train they were hoping to catch was delayed by more than one hour, unless of course it was for reasons that were absolutely exceptional and impossible to forecast.* Although the MPs rejected the Charter on the grounds that they generally drove to work anyway,

* Such as leaves falling down from trees in autumn.

the movement scared them enough to gradually extend the franchise to everyone except Emmeline Pankhurst and the Suffragettes, a late nineteenth-century rock 'n' roll band.

Republicanism in France

As Britain progressed steadily towards democracy, her friendly neighbours across the Channel took an alternative route to political stability: total lawlessness and chaos. With Napoleon out of the way, the leaders of Europe, in one of those rare moments of intuition and vision that reveal with absolute clarity the dangers of smoking opium at international summits, decided to restore the Bourbons to the French throne. It seemed they had momentarily forgotten about the innate tendency of French people to guillotine anyone who even sounded like they might be a brand of biscuits. To be fair, the new Bourbon king, Louis-Philippe, did his best to pretend not to be a Bourbon by dressing up like a banker and calling himself a Citizen. But the quick-witted people were not to be fooled, and on a hot summer's day in 1848 they carefully organised themselves into a rampaging mob and overthrew his failing regime, under the popular democratic slogan 'You're Not as Nice as a Custard Cream'.

This time they got a republic and elected as its first president the nephew of that bastion of popular freedom and human rights . . . Napoleon Bonaparte. Unfortunately, this new ruler, who, to distinguish himself from his illustrious uncle, decided to call himself Napoleon Bonaparte, quickly began to think that not only was he related to Napoleon Bonaparte, he actually *was* Napoleon Bonaparte, a condition the perceptive Sigmund Freud immediately dubbed the 'Napoleon Complex'. He embarked on a series of ridiculous foreign wars, joining conflicts wherever he could find them around the globe, including, at one point, Mexico. Eventually in 1870, he bit off more than he could chew when he was drawn into conflict with Prussia. The Prussians, under Bismarck, promptly marched into Paris and, in an act of magnanimous forbearance, allowed the Parisians to set it on fire themselves.

The French legislature decided they had better elect a new king fast, and, taking a long drag at the opium pipe, concluded that he had better be either a Bourbon or a Bonaparte. Luckily, they were unable to decide which and ended up with another republic instead, France's third. Despite the rule of successive governments being about as dependable as a French marriage vow, the Third Republic somehow clung on and was not snuffed out until Adolf Hitler gave it a quick blow in 1940.

Expansionism in the US

After Britain had generously granted the Americans independence in 1783, the United States had gradually increased her continental territory by a shrewd political tactic known as shopping around at jumble sales. In one of these events, held at a church hall just outside Paris, President Jefferson had been surprised to find, squeezed in between a couple of very attractive pot plants, the state of Louisiana. He immediately put in an offer, as he was very fond of pot plants, and, as a gesture of goodwill, agreed to take Louisiana as well. When he got the bag home, however, he realised that the wily French stall owner had not only given him Louisiana but had slipped in Iowa, Colorado, Kansas and a whole slew of other places too. Although he had no idea where he was going to put them all, Jefferson generously accepted the gift, and from that day American presidents considered it a duty to buy land from whomever was selling it, unless it was the Mexicans, in which case they stole it.

Eventually, however, the country became so big, it began to split in two, with one half being rich, industrialised and free, and the other half being the South. This caused the Civil War, which the North eventually won in 1865 after four years of bitter struggle, in which brother fought against brother, sister fought against sister, and only children got confused. Abraham Lincoln declared that all black people were now to be considered free and equal to their white neighbours, an historic ordinance that was hailed throughout the land, except, of course, in those parts in which black people actually lived.

The terrible destruction of the war left America in dire need of reconstruction. Fortunately, as luck would have it, the very next period in America's history was called the Reconstruction Era. The Reconstruction Era in the north generally took the form of various obscene multimillionaires with made-up surnames like John D. Rockefeller, Andrew Carnegie and Cornelius Wonderwoman. They created monopolies out of oil, steel and railroads, which they would then sell on at a mark-up to the general public, who never quite worked out what they were supposed to do with them. Despite these hiccups, the population of the United States grew exponentially, and by 1900 she had overtaken Britain as the world's largest manufacturer of everything, except cheese and onion crisps.

Test Yourself on the Growth of Liberalism

1. If you created a monopoly out of railroads, how much would your opponents have to pay if they landed on Fenchurch Street Station?

2. Were you ever worried that if you bought both the Electric Company and Waterworks you wouldn't be able to work out how much your opponents owed you if they landed on them with an odd number?

3. Miss Scarlett in the drawing room with the candlestick. Interested?

PART II

NATIONALISM IN ITALY, GERMANY AND RUSSIA

AD 1815–1914

∾

German Unification

In 1870, Europe was thrown into confusion by the sudden announcement that Garibaldi, a red-shirted revolutionary biscuit from Sicily, had just unified Italy. 'What the hell is Italy?' asked the confused Europeans. Then a year later came another shock announcement, this time from the Prussians, along the lines that they were thinking about unifying Germany as well, or at the very least having a lot more wars.

This was not the first time there had been an announcement like that. Romantic revolutionaries had mentioned it back in 1848, only for their unification movement to flounder upon the realisation that it was in danger of being achieved without a full-scale invasion of France. But now the declaration was being made by Otto von Bismarck, Chancellor of Prussia, and that made people take notice. As the key figure of Prussian politics, Bismarck was not primarily interested in unification per se. What he dreamed about at night was furthering the power and prestige of Prussia, which he defined in terms of the number of Prussians living on other people's land. For this, he needed a strong military and lots of wars, and he spent most of his time devising clever plans to provoke his neighbours into declaring them.

His two favourite targets were France and Austria, because they were closest. But first he had to deal with the dangerous rising menace of the Kingdom of Denmark, whose aggressive pastry-making activities sometimes took place quite close to the border. Under Bismarck's persuasion, Austria joined this war too, and together they defeated the marauding bakers of Copenhagen and occupied a good chunk of their land. But joint occupations are always risky, and it was not long before Bismarck had persuaded the Austrians to go to war again, this time against him. With Prussia's military strength the result was never in much doubt, and Bismarck irritated the Austrians from the start by insisting on calling the conflict the Seven Weeks' War. Austria never recovered from the jibe, and Bismarck helped himself to a bunch of northern German states, who pliantly united themselves into a German

Confederation under his leadership.

This left France. As a rule, Bismarck preferred it when states declared war on him rather than the other way round, as it allowed him to seize the moral high ground, where his artillery was more effective. But with Prussia's track record, countries were cottoning on to the fact that this was possibly not a good idea. Fortunately for Bismarck, Napoleon Bonaparte the Stupider had not yet reached the end of his reign.

After several months of diplomatic tension which failed to rouse the young emperor, Bismarck finally found a way to wind him up when he secretly published a telegram in which King William of Prussia politely declined an invitation to meet with the French ambassador. Before releasing it to the press, the wily Chancellor delicately altered the wording, so that instead of the original reading of: 'His Highness King William I regretfully informs the ambassador he will be unable to grant him an audience', it became: 'Napoleon Bonaparte is a big French twat.' The cries of outrage were heard all over France, because the one thing you could never accuse a Bonaparte of was being big. Napoleon immediately declared war, whereupon the Prussian army, which had been quietly massing on the French border for some weeks, marched to Paris and watched the French set it on fire.

With the war over, the rest of the German states decided they'd like to join Prussia's German Confederation too, and thus the second German Reich was born.*

* Alert readers will, of course, remember the first German Reich from Chapter 5. Less alert readers may find it useful to pay attention next time, for Christ's sake.

With French money bankrolling its infrastructure, the new nation was a roaring success, building record numbers of ships, canals and railroads. It was a long time before anyone noticed they all appeared to be pointing towards Belgium.

The Crimean War

As Western Europe succumbed to the hedonistic pleasures of liberalism, capitalism and industry, it was left to Mother Russia to safeguard the traditional values of feudalism, serfdom and mass starvation. Despite a liberal revolt in December 1825 that was so feeble the only name Russians could come up with for it was the December Revolt, the czarist state had continued along its merry way, implementing farsighted decrees such as compulsory twenty-five-year military service, designed to ensure that nobody had time to grow food, ever. They also had a fearsome secret police called the Third Section, who spent their days patrolling the streets of St Petersburg interrogating people who looked like they might know what had happened to Sections One and Two.

In this progressive environment, the Crimean War occurred. This was basically caused by Russia wanting a bit more land, since possessing one-fifth of the world's land mass was clearly not enough for a country whose population had now reached almost a hundred and twenty-six. They chose as their target the Ottoman

Empire, which by this time was so sickly it was receiving round-the-clock care from Florence Nightingale. Fortunately for the Turks, Britain and France waded in on their side, and in a two-year war so comically bad that the suicidal Charge of the Light Brigade was actually celebrated in a poem, the Russians were defeated.

Apart from its great poetry and appalling generalship, the Crimean War was also notable for its journalism, it marking the first time wars had ever been reported upon directly from the front line. Thanks to the pioneering work of William Howard Russell of *The Times*, the people of Britain were able to read at first hand the real story of the Crimean War, before quickly turning to page 3 for what they really wanted to see. It was in fact after reading one of Russell's dispatches from the Battle of Balaclava that Florence Nightingale decided to go to the Crimea, the reporter's descriptions of the barren, lonely conditions the soldiers lived in convincing her that this was a place a single woman could have a seriously good time.*

* Especially if she wore a nurse's costume.

Independence in Latin America

With so much action taking place in their own backyards, it would have been easy for the great European nations to forget that they still had a bunch of hard-working colonies to take care of in Central and South America. Luckily for the hard-working colonies, this is exactly what happened. Haiti gained its independence from France in 1804, while twenty years later Brazil was able to free itself from the evil clutches of Portugal. The only country that really cared about its Latin American colonies was Spain. Unfortunately, by the early nineteenth century this once great Iberian nation had become about as dangerous, in purely military terms, as a rolled-up newspaper. This gave her colonies the chance to strike for freedom.

The first blow was struck by the Argentinians in 1810, when a local man called José de San Martín walked into the city hall in Buenos Aires and announced that he had decided to become the new governor. The startled staff quickly summoned the existing Spanish governor, who, never afraid to back away from a fight, asked the usurper several tough questions about his experience, credentials, etc. before agreeing, reluctantly, to hand over the entire country. At around the same time, a young idealistic hero by the name of Simón Bolívar was hatching a bold plot to take over Colombia. Having planned his campaign down to the finest details, he led an army of three thousand passionate soldiers on an arduous and secret journey over the Andes from Venezuela. His brilliant strategy succeeded in taking the Spanish authorities entirely by surprise, as they were expecting him to take over Colombia by simply showing up with his bus pass.

Separately, these two great leaders made short work of the rest of South America, until San Martín, unwilling to risk the future of the independence movement by coming up against Bolívar, tactfully agreed to die. Simón

Bolívar was thus left with a free hand to rule the fledgling nations, who immediately split into several different territories in order to make themselves ungovernable. After several years of fruitless struggle, Bolívar too decided that on balance the best thing to do would be to pass away, and this he successfully achieved in 1830. It would, however, be the last thing he did, and he never saw Latin America gain the democracy he had spent his life fighting for.

Test Yourself on the Growth of Nationalism

1. Why do you picture the Charge of the Light Brigade as a bunch of men running down a hill with torches in their hands?

2. And why does the Battle of Balaclava remind you of two armed gangs trying to rob a bank at the same time?

PART III

THE AGE OF IMPERIALISM

AD 1815–1914

ᐸᐳ

The Scramble for Africa

Although the European powers gradually lost interest in Latin America, this was not the case with the huge, largely unexplored expanse of Africa. There were, of course, many complex economic, social and religious factors behind the efforts of European explorers to penetrate the so-called dark continent. For example, there were those cool-looking safari hats. Also it was important for Europeans to find out where the source of the River Nile was, just in case it ever came up as a tiebreaker in a pub quiz.

Many early explorers spent years risking everything on this daunting search, before the great Sir Richard Burton, in a typically brilliant moment of scholarly inspiration, suggested they take a look at a map. This helped matters some, but it wasn't until the journalist Henry Morgan Stanley travelled all the way across Central Africa to find David Livingstone and greeted him with the immortal words, 'Sorry, have you any idea how I get to Egypt?' that people realised they had better forget about the source of the Nile for a while, and just get on with the business of stealing all of Africa's silver, gold and diamonds.

This historic decision led to the scramble for Africa, as Britain, France, Germany, Holland, and even, for heaven's sake, Belgium all rushed into the continent, only to crash into each other at the entrance of the Suez Canal. Backing out slowly, they went in again, alphabetically this time, and carefully divided up the proud and ancient continent through complex diplomatic manoeuvring known as playing paper, scissors, stone. This principle worked quite well on the whole, but occasionally the powers did come to blows, notably in the South African Boer War when British and Dutch settlers couldn't agree on who had the prior right to enslave the local black tribespeople.

The rights and wrongs of European imperialism are, of course, still debated today. Certainly many terrible crimes were perpetrated upon the African natives for the benefit of the mother countries. However, it is important to remember that, as well as abuses, the European colonists brought enlightenment, civilisation and sophistication to these backward African nations, providing them with railways, hospitals, churches, schools and other vital public amenities. Sometimes, in the spirit of Victorian philanthropy, they even permitted the Africans to use them.

The Jewel in India's Passage

After Britain had seen off France during one of those unfathomable eighteenth-century wars that took place somewhere on Captain Jenkins' face, she now faced no opposition at all in her bid to rule the massive continent of India, so long as you discounted the two hundred and fifty million Indians themselves, which the British did. Despite the inequality of numbers, the imperial governors quickly won the obedience and respect of their Indian subjects, owing to the Indians' deep and innate appreciation for the fact that the British had guns.

In this way, a continent was gained, and it quickly became the jewel of the British Empire through the negotiation of various fair and mutually beneficial trading deals that the British had learned from the ancient Phoenicians.* The Indians could never quite make up their minds how they thought about their new overlords. On the one hand, they didn't appreciate being treated with condescension and racism in their own country; but on the other hand they did enjoy the look on the British faces when they started bowling leg-spin at them. It wasn't until 1885 that the Indians seriously started to think about independence. But it would be a bitter and non-violent struggle, involving a major Oscar-winning motion picture, before they finally achieved it.[†]

* See page 38.

[†] See page 251.

Handing Out the China

When we last left China, it was 1683 and the Manchus had just taken over the imperial throne. Almost 250 years later, in 1911, the Manchus still had the imperial throne. Unfortunately, everything else in the palace was owned by foreigners.

It was not really the Manchus' fault. They had done their best to keep China healthy and independent by growing moustaches so long they could be used as skipping ropes. But the predilection of many emperors for watching Chinese opera had weakened their ability to stay awake at critical moments. The first of these was the Opium Wars of 1839, when the British sought to make a fair and mutually beneficial trade deal whereby the Chinese would agree to supply the British people with tea leaves and in return the British would supply the Chinese people with harmful and addictive narcotics. This perfectly understandable offer was inexplicably opposed by the Manchus, until the British patiently explained the advantages of the deal by opening fire on their coastline with gunboats. The Chinese, finally getting to grips with the unfamiliar Western logic, quickly agreed to hand over Hong Kong, along with full and exclusive rights to Chris Patten.

This encouraged other major powers to explain their reasoning to the Chinese too, until pretty soon China had become one of the most understanding countries in the whole world. Okinawa and Taiwan went to the Japanese, while the rest of the country was divided up between Britain, France, Germany, Russia and the US. The Chinese, of course, did not mind this a bit, as they had always been rather fond of foreigners, ever since they built a wall to keep them all out. They tried retaliating in 1898 with the Boxer Rebellion, but the foreign powers fought with their gloves off and put the rebels on the canvas in the second round, forcing the Manchus to pay the huge promotion costs. The Chinese dutifully paid up, patiently waiting for the day when they would get their own back by flooding the world with Jackie Chan movies.

The US Gets an Empire, too

By the 1890s, most of the continental United States had been settled, apart from those parts that were clearly uninhabitable.[*] The country was booming, with thriving industries, newly freed slaves and plenty of living space for everyone. It seemed, therefore, like an ideal time to declare war on Spain.

* Such as Washington, DC.

The problem for America was that Spain was a country of white people, and you couldn't just declare war on white people without a very good reason, unless they were French. Fortunately, just at that moment an American warship that had been innocently stationed off the coast of Spanish Cuba inexplicably blew up, killing several important fish. The Spanish immediately protested their innocence, claiming that it couldn't possibly have been them as they had been in Spain at the

Test Yourself on Western Imperialism ∾

1. Counterfactual history: Suppose the Opium Wars had been fought the other way round with the British losing. What impact would this have had on, say, Sunday afternoon meetings of the Mothers' Union?

Would you have been more likely to sign up?

MOTHER'S UNION
WEDNESDAY
SUNDAY.

• WASH YOUR OWN COCAINE INTO CRACK.

• PROTECTING YOUR OPIUM FACTORY

• WHAT SMALL ARMS?

time. But the US refused to take the bait, and in a heroic war that lasted almost as long as it took the Spanish to put their hands up, the Americans crushed the perfidious Iberians and relieved them of their Cuban possession. The Spanish, defiant to the last, refused to accept the terms of their surrender, until America had agreed to take Puerto Rico, Guam, the Philippines and Antonio Banderas from them as well.

The US, flush with its very own empire, announced an important new initiative for the world's foreign policy from then on. Known as the Roosevelt Corollary, it stated that big nations had no right to interfere in the affairs of smaller nations, except in those cases where the big nation happened to be, say, the US, in which case it did. This policy allowed the Americans to non-intervene in places all over the world for years to come. Of course, in the more enlightened times of the twenty-first century the Roosevelt Corollary was replaced by the more sensitive Bush Corollary, which asserted that the US could only interfere in states which posed a genuine and imminent threat to world peace.[*]

* Like Texas.

9.

THE WORLD
ATTEMPTS TO
BLOW ITSELF UP
(AD 1914-1945)

Introduction

How can one sum up the momentous events of the twentieth century? There have been many attempts to describe it: 'the century of war'; 'the century of ideology'; 'the century of science'; 'the century following the nineteenth century'. But all of these pithy phrases fail to give a complete picture of what was, in very real terms, the century that has just finished.

The twentieth century had everything: global wars, great depressions, manic dictators, nuclear bombs, iron curtains, popular revolutions, suicidal terrorists, Russian linesmen, Rod Hull and Emu. It was really just one thing after another, and many people began to wonder if they would ever get to the end of it at all, particularly in the 1980s when luminous socks became popular: But eventually they did get to the end, and they had the fireworks to prove it. Let us begin, then, with the first half of this momentous century, a time of consistent and glorious achievement by the human race, particularly in terms of mass murder.

PART I

THE
FIRST WORLD WAR
AD 1914–1918

෨

The Causes of the War

For some reason, history textbooks always make a
big deal out of the causes of the First World War, as if
this was the first war Europe had ever fought against
herself. The truth was, of course, that Europe had been
in an almost constant state of war with itself, ever
since the day Cro-Magnon man woke up and said, 'You
know, those Neanderthals are really starting to get on
my nerves.' The only remarkable thing about the First
World War was that, through a series of complex and
tortuous alliances that no one could quite follow, France
and Britain somehow found themselves fighting on the
same side.* These same alliances also had Germany
allied with Austro-Hungary, Russia allied with France,
Serbia allied with Russia, Britain allied with Belgium,

* It later
turned out to
have been a
misunderstanding.

France allied with Japan, and Italy allied with whomever happened to be winning at the time.

The alliances were drawn up hastily amid a great deal of customary European tension. Germany and Britain were tense from their race to determine which of the two nations could float the biggest battleship. This was a point of considerable pride for their respective militaries, and there were great celebrations in Britain in 1913 when the Royal Navy fulfilled the dreams of generations and finally succeeded in launching the Isle of Man.* Germany was also tense with France over the fact that she was next door, and with Belgium, over the fact that she was little and defenceless.

Meanwhile, in Austro-Hungary there was tension everywhere, with a secret society called the Black Hand stirring up trouble against them in neighbouring Serbia. The Black Hand, composed of a grand total of ten people, were engaged in a secret plot to unite all the Serbs of Europe into a single empire, even those who didn't actually know they were Serbs. This pre-empted a fateful day in June 1914 when the heir to the Austro-Hungarian empire, Archduke Franz Ferdinand, wandered carelessly into Sarajevo just as a young Black Hand operative called Gavrilo Princip was planning to assassinate John F. Kennedy. Unfortunately, the bullet hit the Archduke instead, thus giving Germany no choice but to launch an immediate invasion of Belgium.

Before that happened, Austro-Hungary declared war on Serbia, Russia declared war on Austro-Hungary,

---

* Successfully drowning a great many offshore bankers.

France joined sides with Russia, Germany joined sides with Austro-Hungary, Britain joined sides with France, and Italy, extremely confused, declared war on herself, whereupon she quickly surrendered. It was 4 August 1914.

The Course of the War

Everybody was sure that the First World War would be over by Christmas, and indeed it was. Just not Christmas 1914. The reason it lasted so long, of course, was because of the tendency of soldiers on both sides to jump out of their trenches at regular intervals in order to play football in no-man's-land, a proclivity that eventually prompted military commanders to scuff up their pitch with shell holes. The other reason was because of tactics.

In previous wars, battles had been over quickly owing to a slight but significant technical flaw in the guns the soldiers used, i.e. they didn't work. The accepted formula for winning a battle was, therefore, to run as fast as you could at the enemy troops, stop a few metres short of their front line, take cover, and then wait expectantly for their muskets to blow up in their faces.

In the First World War, however, defending armies managed to develop a new kind of weapon called the machine gun, which threatened to upset the odds completely. The machine gun was not only capable of firing bullets in the right general direction but could do so six hundred times every minute. Clearly running straight at the enemy in such circumstances would be suicidal, if not downright dangerous, and so the crack military generals of Europe quickly got together to devise a brilliant new strategy for attacking the enemy's defences. Led by the visionary Field Marshal Haig, they decided that, instead of running straight at the enemy's front lines, their soldiers should now *walk* instead, preferably extremely slowly and in a straight line. This bold new tactic took defending armies entirely by surprise, and on some days attacking forces were able to advance two or even three metres in succession before the enemy machine-gunners could stop laughing. Wilfred Owen and other war poets memorialised these glorious events in verse:

> And lo, as the fiery fingers of dawn
> Reach out across the mud of Flanders fields,
> The cry 'Advance!' issues through the –
> Uuurgh.

It was four years before anyone realised the total insanity of this strategy, but by then it was too late because the war was over. As everyone knows, it was decided that for poetry's sake the final bullet should be fired on exactly the eleventh hour of the eleventh day of the eleventh month of the year. It was only misfortune that the decision did not reach the ears of Private William Burke of the 27th British Infantry who, having proceeded to fire another bullet shortly after eleven o'clock, inadvertently caused the war to continue for an entire extra year.

The Treaty of Versailles

During the long years of hell from 1914 to 1918, people had taken to calling the terrible, bloody conflict The War To End All Wars. After the Treaty of Versailles was signed in 1919, they realised they ought to change its name to the First World War.

The discussion over how to treat the defeated nations ranged around the Fourteen Points drawn up by US president Woodrow Wilson. This enlightened document proposed that:

1. The victorious nations should treat the losers with dignity and moderation, and refrain, for example, from stripping them of huge amounts of money and land.
2. Disputes between nations from now on should be settled not by war but earnest discussion and mutual understanding.
3. Men should not be embarrassed to cry in public.

Britain and France listened to the American president's ideas carefully, painstakingly debating them one by one, until by the end they were laughing so hard they almost ruptured their parliaments. In the end, they decided that on the whole they would in fact quite like to strip the losers of huge amounts of money and land, for otherwise how would they pay for the armaments they would need to build when the humiliated Germans inevitably rose up in revenge?

They did, however, agree to start a League of Nations, which, after the first round of games, was being comfortably led by Britain, with Germany a pretty firm last. The US elected not to join, forming their own domestic league instead with only themselves as members. The winners of the US league still called themselves World Champions.

Test Yourself on the First World War

1. Where, in an average British garden, would you be most likely to find a Woodrow?

2. How about a Bush?

PART II

THE RISE OF DICTATORS

AD 1917–1939

❧

The Russian Revolution

Russia, always a happy-go-lucky place at the worst of times, got even better with the coming of the First World War. Russian peasants, enjoying their first day off work since around 1683, were provided with free travel to Poland, where they were offered semi-permanent accommodation inside shell holes, a significant grade up on their usual abodes. They were practically unbeatable in battle, since the army had equipped them with the most advanced weaponry Russia had available. The soldiers made these weapons even more effective by crushing them together in their hands until they were almost like iceballs. It was said that the best snipers could pick out a German helmet from fifteen paces.

The Russians were fearless in battle, inspired by the brilliance of their supreme commanders, Tzar Nicholas II and his beautiful wife Rasputin. But despite all their courage, the war did not go well, and by 1917 many of the soldiers had decided they just didn't want to play any more. Meanwhile, in the city of Petrograd, Bolshevik agitators had been inciting the local populace into starting food riots. Although the city lent its name to a particularly useful expression, and the riots quickly 'petered out' when the Bolsheviks realised that the local populace didn't actually have any food to riot with, it was enough to encourage an exiled Marxist radical called Lenin to return to his homeland in order to promote revolution. This he achieved on 7 November 1917, under the popular slogan of 'Peace, Bread, and Siberian Labour Camps'.

A civil war followed, which the Communists eventually won after Lenin had the Tzar and his family brutally stabbed to death with his beard. The Bolsheviks took control, and celebrated the founding of their free socialist workers' paradise by creating a secret police to make sure nobody could ever leave. In 1924, Lenin died, leaving his good friend Trotsky to take over. But Trotsky decided all of a sudden that he would rather get secretly murdered with an ice pick in Mexico. (So now you know the answer to the perennial question 'Whatever happened to Leon Trotsky?') Then lots of other Soviet leaders suddenly decided that they too would rather get secretly murdered, until eventually there was only one Soviet leader left. He, of course, had had nothing personally to do with any of these secret murders, a fact he proved conclusively by secretly murdering anyone who suggested he did. His name was Joseph Stalin and he had grand ideas for Mother Russia, including an ambitious Five-Year Plan to starve her entire population to death.

The Rise of Mussolini

In Italy after the First World War, there was a great deal of confusion, squabbling and unrest. However, in many other respects, the situation was quite abnormal. The main problem was the economy, which was depressed. It was thinking: 'For Christ's sake, why do I have to be the economy of Italy?'* Also depressed were the unemployed Italian soldiers returning from the war, angry that, despite winning many valiant victories against themselves, they had not got anything out of the Versailles settlement.

One of these returning soldiers was a rotund corporal by the name of Benito Mussolini. Unable to find a proper job in the bleak workplace, the young firebrand joined up with bands of disaffected soldiers to form *fascisti* gangs, whose idea of a good time was to roam the streets in threatening black shirts and try, if at all possible, not to spill bolognese sauce down them. This was far from an easy task to accomplish, and eventually the hapless Italian government began to think that

* The economy of Ireland has similar psychological issues.

MUSSOLINI — SO BIG HE COULD SWALLOW
HIS ENEMIES WHOLE.

Mussolini might be the kind of man the country needed
to lead it down a road of complete devastation and ruin.
In 1922, King Victor Emmanuel III invited him to form a
government, under the stipulation that he should not on
any account dispose of his political enemies and set up
a vicious, bloodthirsty dictatorship, at least for a couple
of years or so.

He was forgetting, of course, that Mussolini had no need
to dispose of his enemies, since he was a big enough man
simply to swallow them whole. As the all-powerful *Duce*
of Italy, he cultivated the image of the tireless superman,
though where Superman flew Mussolini tended to roll.
He managed to revive the economy through massive
state building projects, mainly of statues of himself, and
fattened the government coffers by encouraging citizens

to send in their gold jewellery so that it could be melted down and made into chocolate. However, he left the railways well alone. Fact.

By 1935, however, he was bored, and it dawned on him that if he was going to be remembered as a truly great leader he needed to lead Italy to glory in some pointless foreign conquest. Alas, this meant finding a pointless foreign conquest that Italy could realistically win, which left Mussolini with a choice of either a defenceless country somewhere in Africa, or the Vatican City. In the end he plumped for Abyssinia, but, even so, quickly found his troops held back by the fearsome African soldiers, many of whom had spears. It took a sustained bombing campaign with chemical weapons to subdue the natives, but finally Italy had her colony. Mussolini's legacy was assured.

The Rise of Japan

Meanwhile, on the other side of the world, Japan was beginning to make its presence felt. Up until now, the little island nation had been mainly known for the varied and inventive ways its citizens had found to kill themselves, the latest craze being long and sustained exposure to painful amateur singing. But as the twentieth century dawned, the Japanese had decided that if they were going to expend vast creative energy in killing themselves, they might as well start taking other nations with them, too.

They began in 1905 with a neat little war with Russia, but before long had turned their attentions to China, which by the 1920s had become like a vast beached whale, ready to be carved up and eaten. Japan, never one to turn down a whale hunt, had already established a strong garrison in Manchuria, and now she seized the province outright. The League of Nations responded in typically forthright style by sending the aggressors a stern letter of protest, which the Japanese folded into an elaborate paper crane and floated down a river.

A few years later, in 1937, they expanded beyond Manchuria and embarked upon a full-scale invasion of China after being gratuitously provoked by Chinese terrorists, who were clearly overheard making a joke about bonsai. The war was fought with the honour born of Japan's code of *bushido*, epitomised by the behaviour of the Japanese soldiers upon the fall of Nanjing when they generously agreed to leave at least two of the town's civilians alive. After this, however, the Chinese began to conduct a guerrilla war against the invaders, and the conflict settled into a bloody stalemate.

The Rise of Little Adolf

In the small Austrian town of Braunau in 1889, a young whippersnapper by the name of Adolf came into the world. A popular child at school, owing to his amusing moustache and hilarious array of joke salutes, Adolf grew up wanting to be an artist. Travelling to

Vienna as a young man, he attempted to enter the prestigious Academy of Art, only to find that it had bizarre, prejudicial biases against people with no talent. Scraping a living as a postcard artist, he was forced to live among the poorest dregs of Viennese society. Here he developed an irrational hatred of Jewish people, based mainly on their ability to grow large, impressive beards which made his own 'Hitler moustache' appear woefully inadequate.*

In 1914 the war came, and Hitler enrolled in the army. He distinguished himself on the front lines by sitting in the trenches and regaling his comrades with long maniacal tirades against all the different kinds of people in the world he had a grudge against, up to and including milkmen. He was a brave soldier, however, and frequently risked his life on daring missions to no-man's-land, something his comrades encouraged whenever possible.

When the war ended in the humiliation of Versailles, he gravitated to Munich where he found acceptance as a rabble-rousing speaker in the beer halls. By 1923, he had taken over as leader of the National Socialist German Workers' Party, which, as its name suggested, was generally made up of right-wing, unemployed Austrians. In that year, Hitler led the party on an unsuccessful putsch in Munich, for which he was imprisoned for a year. During this time, he penned *Mein Kampf*, a moving account of his inability to sustain an erection, translated as *My Struggle*.

* Hitler later tried to force all the Jews to shave, a measure he called the First Solution.

When he was released, he set about rebuilding and expanding his fledgling party, and was given a huge boost in 1929 when the Great Depression suddenly made depraved spit-emitting lunatics seem like visionaries. The Nazis began to win more and more seats in the Reichstag, and by 1932 had become the biggest party in Germany. In January 1933, President von Hindenburg, taking a break from his daytime role as an airship, invited the young firebrand to be Chancellor, assuming that giving him a free ticket to unlimited power would be the best way to keep him under control. But, although Hitler had many qualities, control was certainly not one of them, and he set about losing it repeatedly until eventually he got so hot under the collar he accidentally burned down the Reichstag. Deciding to call himself the *Führer* – or 'Monstrous One-Balled Madman' – he began to rule as a dictator.

Test Yourself on the Rise of Dictators

1. Have we had enough jokes about facial hair yet? Explain.

2. How about jokes about Germans?

PART III

THE
SECOND WORLD WAR
AD 1939-1945

ৡৎ

The Road to War

With the benefit of hindsight, it would be easy to suggest that war was inevitable the moment Adolf Hitler came to power. But hindsight, of course, was not available to the Western European leaders at the time. They had to make do with nothing but their own innate blindness and stupidity.

Events began to overtake them in 1936 when Hitler invaded the Rhineland. The Rhineland was technically part of France, but the French wisely elected not to fight back just in case the Germans had brought guns.[*] Then came the Spanish Civil War, fought between the nationalist troops of General Franco on one side and Ernest Hemingway on the other. Hitler intervened on Franco's side, and tested out his fearsome new Luftwaffe

[*] They hadn't.

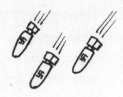

THE SPANISH CIVIL WAR – THE LUFTWAFFE
CARPET-BOMBING CAMPAIGN OF HEMINGWAY
NOVELS CAUSED A GREAT DEAL OF UNNECCESSARY
PUNCTUATION.

on several of Hemingway's heavyweight novels, causing a great deal of unnecessary punctuation.

This brought the world to 1938, which was marked by the Munich conference, an attempt by the Western powers to persuade Hitler not to invade more than about half of Czechoslovakia. To their great delight, Hitler agreed, at least to the invasion part, and British prime minister Neville Chamberlain stepped off his plane excitedly waving a piece of paper containing Hitler's autograph. 'It's peace in our time!' he declared in demented fashion, apparently unaware that what Hitler had actually said was '*Peas* in our time', a reference to Poland's major cash crop.

A year later, Hitler duly invaded Poland, having first signed a non-aggression pact with Stalin in which he agreed not to attack the Soviet Union until he was ready. Britain and France reluctantly declared war. It was 3 September 1939.

The War

France was confident that the war would be over by Christmas, but most other observers doubted that it would hold out that long against the Hun. The Germans invaded through Belgium, as dictated by their constitution, and immediately caused a panic among British tourists in Dunkirk who were waiting forlornly for the ferry strike to end. From then on, things went very badly for the Allies. The Germans, trying to soften the British up for an invasion, began to drop bombs on London, guided unerringly towards their target by the unearthly sound of Vera Lynn's singing. In those dark times, caused largely by blackouts, new prime minister Winston Churchill urged his countrymen to carry on their lives as normal: 'We shall fight on the beaches,' he intoned gravely. 'We shall fight in the fields and in the streets, in the bars and the kebab houses, and outside the pubs at closing time. And also before and after football matches, naturally.' The Germans wisely called off the invasion.

Elsewhere in the world, Hitler had decided that Germany was in severe danger of winning the war, and

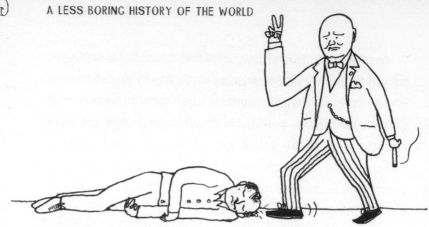

'WE SHALL FIGHT IN THE FIELDS AND IN THE STREETS, IN BARS AND OUTSIDE KEBAB SHOPS. AND BEFORE, AND AFTER, FOOTBALL MATCHES.'

so decided to invade Russia to even up the odds. Even this, however, failed to stem the tide, as the blitzkrieg quickly rolled into the outskirts of Moscow. He was only saved from embarrassment by the Japanese, who, having found their conquest of Asia rather too straightforward so far, realised that the only way they were going to be able to kill themselves in large enough numbers was if they brought America into the war. They did this by launching a surprise attack on America's naval base at Pearl Harbor, a dastardly and cowardly act that outraged the Americans, mainly because they hadn't thought of something dastardly like that first. The attack gave the Japanese the opportunity to produce units of crack kamikaze pilots, who would spend several years honing their skills at flight school before eventually taking control of their feared Zero fighter planes and crashing them deliberately into the sea.

In the end, the strategy of the Axis powers began to pay off. In 1943, mathematicians at Bletchley Park were able to begin reading the secret Nazi naval communications when, with a mixture of brilliant intuition and pure blind luck, they stumbled upon a German–English dictionary. This enabled analysts to learn the location of the feared Nazi U-boats, which had been hounding Allied shipping persistently since 1939. 'They're underwater,' the analysts said.

By June 1944, the Allies were ready to launch a counter-attack. In order to confuse the Germans as to the exact location of the invasion, they decided to advertise it as the Normandy landings, thinking, rightly, that the Germans would assume it was a trick and immediately remove all their troops from Normandy. When it turned out not to be a trick, the Allies were able to land their troops successfully and advance towards Paris, where, in a moment of confusion, the French surrendered unconditionally. From then on, it was only a matter of time before Germany fell, and on 30 April 1945 Hitler made his only sensible decision of the war and committed suicide in his bunker.

Japan continued to hold out, however, promising to resist until every last one of her citizens was dead. Eventually America, afraid of the very real possibility that this wasn't a joke, felt compelled to unleash a devastating new weapon on their unsuspecting enemy, a tool of war so hideous and destructive the Japanese would have no choice but to surrender.

Walt Disney films.

The ruthless dropping on Hiroshima and Nagasaki of sickly animated movies like *Bambi* was the final straw for the exhausted citizens of Japan. On 15 August 1945, Emperor Hirohito spoke to his people for the very first time and announced, with the kind of outrageous overstatement he was renowned for, that 'the war had not developed necessarily to Japan's advantage', prompting his heartbroken nation to immediately set about conquering the world with PlayStation instead.

The United Nations

With sixteen million soldiers dead and tens of millions still alive, it was generally agreed by the major powers that the Second World War had not altogether been a good thing. Towards the end of the war, therefore, they got together in various obscure-sounding places in order to discuss ways they could prevent it happening again, at least until they could do it properly with nuclear weapons. The outcome of these discussions was the United Nations. The UN came into being in April 1945 at San Francisco, for, if you were going to pick a place to discuss love for your fellow man, San Francisco was clearly the obvious choice.

The UN was divided into a General Assembly and a Security Council. In the General Assembly, nations of all sizes, no matter how weak or embarrassing, could come together and vote equally in favour of whichever major power had recently given them the most aid. The Security Council, on the other hand, only had the world's most powerful countries, plus France. Its role was to work towards democracy and world peace by issuing strong, binding resolutions that could then be ignored by all the countries involved. Both of these institutions continue to perform these important functions today.

Test Yourself on the Second World War

1. 'A date which will live in infamy' (Franklin D. Roosevelt). What were you doing on the day *Pearl Harbor* came out at the cinema?

2. Complete this famous saying by Winston Churchill: 'Madam, I may be very drunk but you are very ugly. At least in the morning I shall be _____.' (a) sober (b) incontinent (c) in bed with a horse.

10.

THE END OF
THE WORLD
(AD 1945-present day)

Introduction

As the world entered the second half of the twentieth century, it had a whole new set of problems to face. Hitler and Mussolini might have been out of the way, but that did not mean there were no more deranged psychopaths lurking dangerously in the shadows. Indeed, Jeremy Beadle lasted well into the next century and, according to some religions, may well still rise again. For the first forty years of the post-war era, the world's attention was occupied by a frosty nuclear standoff between East and West, which allowed colonial nations in Africa, India and the Middle East to sneakily claim independence while no one was looking. Then, just as one arch enemy of the West fell, another rose in the form of vengeful Islamic terrorists, who blamed decadent Western morals for the dramatic reduction in beards throughout the world. Shattering atrocities followed, including the Lockerbie bombing, the attack on the World Trade Center, the Madrid train bombings, and – worst of all for Britain and its long-suffering capital – the London congestion charge.

PART I

ROCKY VS DRAGO
AD 1945–2000

❦

The Cold War

At the end of the Second World War, the victorious Allied nations of Britain, America and the Soviet Union agreed that, in order to reduce the risk of a future conflict involving Germany and Japan, they should now turn their attention towards having one with each other. Stalin was so concerned about the future security of his nation that he created a small buffer zone to protect it, consisting of the nations of Poland, Czechoslovakia, East Germany, Hungary, Bulgaria, Romania, Latvia, Lithuania, Estonia, Yugoslavia, Albania, Georgia and Ukraine. The Soviets allowed these countries to hold free and democratic elections in which, after much debate and discussion, they voted in favour of not getting shot by the KGB. The result was that the world was now divided into two camps, one dominated by dangerous, psychologically unstable megalomaniacs and the other by the Russians.

For the next forty years, these two camps desperately tried to outdo each other in every field of human endeavour, such as revolution-starting, missile-building, space exploration and tedious adult board games. The climax of the board game rivalry was reached in a classic chess confrontation between Bobby Fischer and Boris Spassky in 1972, which kept the world enthralled for over three months, by which time both players had managed to complete their opening moves. The space race also witnessed some great contests, most notably in the fight to send the first man to the moon. This fight took place, of course, on the stairs of the landing module of Apollo 11, and has been immortalised in the words of Buzz Aldrin as he prepared to take the first step on to the lunar surface: 'One small step for man, one giant leap for – Ow! What the — ? Oh, you sneaky *bastard*, Armstrong!'

The other great confrontation took place in 1962 and was known as the Cuban Missile Crisis. This was caused when the leader of Cuba, Fidel Castro, invited the Russians to come to his island to build a new high-class beach resort. The resort was to be equipped with all the latest Communist luxuries and comforts, such as flushing toilets and live nuclear warheads. The Americans, however, were upset, for if anyone was going to build a high-class beach resort in Cuba they wanted it to be men they could trust, like the mafia. After twelve days' anxious dithering in which they argued back and forth between the two alternatives of either solving the crisis diplomatically or starting a nuclear war, President Kennedy eventually ordered a naval blockade to stop the Russians getting through. But the Soviets refused to back down, and as their ships continued to plough their way towards Cuba, the whole world held its breath to see whether they would suddenly disappear inside the Bermuda Triangle.

Fortunately, they just turned round and went home instead, and the earth suddenly seemed a warmer place. The 1970s were a time of détente, as Richard Nixon ordered his trusty henchmen to break into the Watergate building and the Russians realised they did have something in common with the Americans after all. This was the beginning of the famous summits between the two nations, which continued into the premierships of Reagan and Gorbachev. President Reagan's Cold War policy was based on a long-term, strategic plan known, in top-level diplomatic circles, as his wife's horoscope. The Horoscope Doctrine allowed the president to go into these vital summits fully briefed on the likely impact there would be on international affairs if the planet Mars happened to come into alignment with, say, the huge mark on Gorbachev's head. In this way, the Soviets gradually came to see that there really wasn't all that much to fear from their great capitalist adversary, and the Cold War slowly grew to a close.

"One small step for man, one giant leap for – Ow! What the – ? Oh, you sneaky bastard, Armstrong!"

War in Korea

After Japan's defeat in 1945, the peninsula of Korea was divided along the 38th parallel into Soviet and American zones of occupation. By 1948, these zones had become formalised as separate countries: a Communist north and a capitalist south. The inevitable war began two years later, when the North Korean army decided, with the weather turning a bit colder, that it would quite like to spend its summer holiday that year on the south coast. The result was a horrible, messy conflict that was propped up on one side by the US and on the other by China, and which ended up in exactly the same position from which it started. The American war strategy was hampered continually by their mobile MASH units, which offered such high-quality humour and entertainment, not to mention nurses, that many infantrymen went into battle with the explicit intention of becoming actors.

War in Vietnam

If the Korean war was nasty, its hand-picked successor in Vietnam was almost Rambo-like in its awfulness. With a monotonous setting, a young inexperienced cast and an absurd and gratuitous plot, it was a box-office disaster, so violently unpopular in the country of its making that young people were driven to reject it in favour of peace marches, LSD parties, and even – horrifyingly – sitar music. So etched into the American consciousness has the war become that presidential candidates can still not get through an election campaign without tearfully explaining what a terrifying and life-changing experience it would have been for them had daddy not paid for them to get out of it.*

So, what was the Vietnam War all about? Well, that was not something most people were very clear about, least of all the American troops, most of whom were so stoned they assumed they must still be back in the 'hood. Confused about who they were meant to be fighting for or against, the Americans resorted to the tactic of attacking everything, up to and including foliage. Eventually things got so bad they elected Richard Nixon, who, if nothing else, could at least be trusted to sell the South Vietnamese down the river. This he duly achieved in 1973, and two years later Saigon fell.

* The honourable exception to this, of course, is Senator John McCain, who was so badly tortured as a POW in Vietnam, he almost went sane.

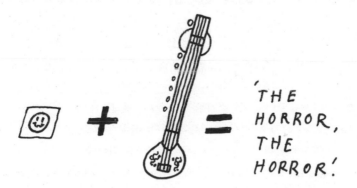

THE WAR IN VIETNAM: VIOLENTLY REJECTED IN FAVOUR OF PEACE MARCHES, LSD PARTIES AND SITAR MUSIC.

The Fall of the Soviet Union

At midnight on 9 November 1989, people all over the world turned on their TV sets and were treated to the extraordinary sight of thousands of East Berliners clambering over the wall that divided their city. A few seconds later, the people turned off their television sets, because, quite frankly, they had been looking for late-night porn. But they quickly realised the significance of the event they had witnessed: Germany was at last, after all these years and against all the odds, finally invading itself.

The fall of the Berlin Wall did not occur in isolation. Walls in the Eastern bloc had actually been falling down regularly for several years due to the fact that most of the builders had been exiled to Siberia. This had prompted President Gorbachev to enact much-needed economic and political reforms in the region, known as *Glasnost* and er . . . you know, that other one, *Pere—*something. Suddenly, after years of only being able to write what the Communist government told them to, the press in Russia found itself with the freedom to say what it wanted. Soon the Soviet bloc was reeling at the news that Angelina Jolie and Brad Pitt were having relationship problems, and was stunned to hear that, contrary to the lies told them by the Communists, Elvis was still alive and living in Albania.

Gorbachev did not stand a chance. In August 1991, he was overthrown by a hardline KGB coup. Although

THE FALL OF THE SOVIET UNION

the plot failed after three days, having slightly misread the nation's mood, Gorbachev was soon overthrown again, this time by the huge figure of Boris Yeltsin. Yeltsin had started out as a supporter of the president, until he had been alienated by a government drive against alcoholism. Once he was in power he quickly set about destroying the last remnants of the Soviet Union. On 25 December 1991, the Soviet flag was lowered from the Kremlin for the last time, and was replaced by a large golden M.

Test Yourself on Rocky vs Drago

1. Can you name any other former world leaders with unsightly or unsettling birthmarks? (*Hint: Gordon Brown's face*)

PART II

INDEPENDENCE AND REVOLUTION

AD 1945-2000

ᕽᖇ

Independence for India

Meanwhile, in other parts of the world, history was taking place in sporadic fashion too. In India the word of the day was independence.

The movement for independence was led by Mohandas Gandhi, a small Hindu holy man whose mind was so focused on liberating his country from the British that he kept forgetting to put on his shoes. Gandhi based his philosophy on the precept of non-violence, which he used as a weapon against his British overlords. To the British, who had certainly heard of violence before but had never thought to combine it with a prefix, this was an utterly perplexing tactic. Although some of them actually had sympathy for Gandhi's cause, they couldn't quite trust the Indians to govern themselves, being inexperienced, ill-educated and brown. The only response to the independence movement they could think of was to put all of Gandhi's supporters in prison, 60,000 in a matter of weeks at one point. The Indians were understandably outraged by this, until they remembered that in the First World War the British had managed to kill that number of their own people in a single day.

Eventually, however, the British had little choice but to give in. For although Gandhi's body was slight, his voice was loud enough to carry across continents, echoing even in the corridors of Westminster. With the time difference, politicians found it was even disturbing their sleep. In 1947, they finally granted India her independence. Unfortunately, bleary from lack of sleep, they also decided at the last minute to divide the territory into two, with a Hindu India and a Muslim Pakistan, and placed Kashmir conveniently close to both so that they would always have something to fight over. The situation remains largely the same today, except that now both countries have nuclear weapons so that if one side does ever manage to win the region decisively nobody will be able to live there anyway.*

* It is also important not to forget the nation of Bangladesh which was established in the same region in 1971, for some reason.

Problems in Africa

Independence for the nations of Africa was similarly troubled, owing to a tiny administrative oversight made when the national boundaries were drawn up.† In the rush to colonise the dark continent, the imperial powers

† In that they were completely random.

had not really considered the idea that the disparate tribes of Africa might not actually *want* to live together in the same country. The colonialists thought that, despite their deep historical divisions of language, culture and ethnicity, the tribes would eventually start, if not to like each other, then at least vaguely tolerate each other's existence, rather like the English and the Welsh. The reality, however, was rather different. As a result, tribal conflicts dominated many of the new nations, with Muslim Arabs fighting Christian Nilotics in Sudan, southern Bantus fighting northern Nilotics in Uganda, and Ovimbundus fighting Kimbundus and Bakongos in Angola. This paved the way for a succession of vicious military dictators to seize control, such as Idi Amin, who was so mad even the British eventually stopped doing deals with him.

In the 1980s, civil war, along with failed harvests and drought, led to the greatest danger of all for the beleaguered continent: Bob Geldof. Suddenly, as if it was not overpopulated enough, Africa found itself besieged by tens of thousands of well-meaning pop stars, who would look down sorrowfully at the poor, starving children of Ethiopia before proceeding to torment them with songs about Christmas. To its credit, Live Aid woke the world up to the unfolding catastrophe on the continent, generating a vast outpouring of charity and help. It didn't succeed, however, in finding a cure for Bob Geldof.

Trouble in Latin America

The story of the American continent after 1945 was one of corrupt leaders, cruel suppression of civil rights and ruthless, unprincipled exploitation of common people. But there were problems south of the United States border, too.

In Central America, there was the problem of vile, wicked socialists attempting to win elections, which forced the United States to keep sending over parties of marines in order to keep the countries safe for honest, democratic citizens, like the United Fruit Company. Most notably came the infamous Iran–Contra affair in 1986, when President Reagan, in an act so secret even the KGB largely kept it to themselves, gave permission for the CIA to sell American arms to Iran in order to fund anti-government rebels in Nicaragua. This became a big scandal, because (a) Iran was America's greatest enemy, who had recently taken lots of her embassy staff hostage, and (b) people hadn't realised there was a government in Nicaragua. It ended in congressional hearings, at which President Reagan persuaded the American people that he could not possibly have known about the affair by claiming – quite convincingly – that he hadn't been aware he even *was* the president. It turned out that he thought the president was Colonel Oliver North, who later proved it conclusively by being convicted of several major felonies without going to prison.

Further south in the continent, there were similar ups and downs. Brazil endured a difficult military dictatorship before emerging, triumphantly and against expectation, as winners of the 2002 World Cup. Now a fully fledged democracy, it has made great strides in economic and environmental spheres, ridding the world of vast stretches of dangerous Amazon rainforest, which had contained many quite unpleasant bugs. Chile also suffered a dictatorship under General Pinochet, who tortured and imprisoned at least 28,000 people while safeguarding the country against democracy. Until his recent death, Chile repeatedly sought to prosecute the former ruler, on several charges of being very old and decrepit.

Then there was Argentina. Nobody in Britain had been aware of the existence of Argentina until the 1980s when, without warning or provocation, the corrupt military government, seeking a nationalist cause with which to silence their opposition in the country, in 1986 ordered Maradona to score a goal with his hand. This was in revenge for Britain's sinking of the *Belgrano* in the Falklands War four years earlier. Apart from that, Argentinian history followed the usual South American pattern of failed democracy and military juntas, interrupted only by Eva Perón's plaintive song to her nation, 'Don't Cry For Me, Argentina', to which Argentina, still proud, replied: 'It's My Party and I'll Cry if I Want To.'

Revolution in China

During the Japanese invasion of China in the 1930s, the Nationalist party under Chiang Kai-shek and the Communists under Mao Zedong had put aside their differences to fight the hated invaders. When the Japanese left in 1945, however, they quickly put their differences back together and had a civil war. Mao won this, forcing Chiang to flee to Taiwan, where he embarked on a long-term plot to bring down his populous neighbour by having his country mass-produce small plastic toys that mainland children would put in their mouths and choke on.

Mao, meanwhile, concentrated on making China prosperous and advanced by forcing everybody to wear ill-fitting, collarless beige suits. In 1958, he ordered the Great Leap Forward, which aimed to revitalise the backward Chinese countryside by preventing peasants from growing any food. Strangely, this resulted in widespread famine, eventually forcing Mao to abandon his ambitious Five-Year Plan in favour of a Four-Year Plan of never brushing his teeth and occasionally going for a swim.

Once the Four-Year Plan was over, however, he decided it was time to take control again. He announced the launch of the Cultural Revolution, in which the tired intellectual establishment of old China was to be swept aside in favour of a new wave of fresh and energetic leaders, known in the techno-speak of Communist China as schoolchildren. These leaders quickly set out

In 1958, he ordered the Great Leap Forward, which aimed to revitalise the backward Chinese countryside by preventing peasants from growing any food.

their ambitious agenda for the country, directing the government apparatus towards the implementation of important new initiatives to modernise China, such as abolishing early bedtimes and forcing teachers to wear silly hats. All free-thinking adults were at risk. But as they were dragged off to be re-educated in the labour camps, they consoled themselves with the thought that sooner or later Chinese families would only be permitted to have one child each.

Test Yourself on Independence and Revolution

1. One child, one family. A frustrating measure for the people of China?

PART III

THE WORLD TODAY

Israel and the Middle East

Amongst all the terrible crimes committed during the Second World War,* the most horrifying had undoubtedly been the Nazi extermination of the Jews. These unspeakable events had persuaded European leaders that the Jewish people needed to be given a homeland, a place where they could live in safety without fear of hatred or persecution. Obviously Europe was out of the question for this homeland and Newt Gingrich had not yet built his moon colony. There was, therefore, only one place left. And so it was that on the historic day of 14 May 1948, Jews from all over the world finally returned to the Middle East where, full of hope, they began to build their homes in the brand new state of Israel, just about twenty-four hours before their Arab neighbours started bombarding them with shells.

It turned out that, due to a slight cartographical oversight, there hadn't actually been any space for Israel in the Middle East, and creating it had involved performing a hysterectomy on Palestine. This was something that

* Such as the movie *Windtalkers*.

one or two Arab nations, such as – to take an example at random – all of them, were not terribly pleased about. War was the inevitable result. Fortunately for Israel, the Arabs were still in their post-independence infancy and possessed the combined military strength of a single American daycare nursery. Whatever they tried always ended in humiliation, culminating in the comically one-sided Six Day War by the end of which Israel had occupied the Sinai Peninsula, the Gaza Strip, the Golan Heights, the West Bank and the whole of Jerusalem.

Eventually things got so embarrassing that even the Americans felt they had to intervene. In 1978, President 'Jimmy' Carter invited the Israeli and Egyptian leaders to Camp David for a secret conference. There was a great deal of nervousness in both parties as they arrived at

A CAMP DAVID DELEGATE.

Camp David, for everyone knew that Carter would not let them leave until he had made them listen to his entire collection of peanut farming anecdotes. Indeed, the conference dragged on for thirteen long days. But eventually Carter's dogged Southern negotiating skills got through to the embittered men, and they committed suicide. Just before that, however, he managed to get them to sign the Camp David Accords, in which the two nations agreed to remain at peace just as long as Carter agreed not to call them when they got home.

This, however, did not solve the crisis in the Middle East. In 1979, the Western world was stunned by the seizure of power by an unpredictable, extremist lunatic who threatened to overthrow the entire balance of power. Then Ayatollah Khomeini took power in Iran, and people turned their attention away from Margaret Thatcher and back to the Middle East. The Islamic Revolution presented the West with a whole new set of problems, and they were relieved when their friendly, dependable ally Saddam Hussein stepped in to start the Iran–Iraq War.

The First Gulf War

Unfortunately, the situation in Iraq didn't turn out as well as the West had hoped. A few years after the Iran–Iraq war, the West suddenly discovered that, far from being the firm but benevolent dictator they thought he was, Saddam Hussein turned out to want to keep the region's oil supplies for himself. When Saddam invaded Kuwait in 1990, half the world came out against him.

The first Gulf War was widely regarded to be justified on account of it making really excellent television. With camera-mounted weapons and flak-jacket-mounted reporters, it introduced the world to technological marvels like Patriot missiles, as well as the occasional Scud, which the Americans would launch from their bases in Saudi Arabia and, with unerring accuracy, shoot down British helicopters. Unfortunately, they were never quite as accurate when they aimed at Saddam Hussein himself and, despite looking more and more like Stavros by the hour, the sturdy old warrior lived to fight another day.

Palestinian Terror

Saddam Hussein was not the only danger coming out of the Middle East. The 1970s saw the start of the Palestinian intifada, under the towering leadership of Mount Arafat. Determined to win their homeland back, the Palestinians began to look to the wider international community for support, selling their peaceful campaign for justice by hijacking passenger aeroplanes and blowing up restaurants. In 1972, the splinter group Black September kidnapped and massacred eleven Israeli athletes at the Munich Olympics in a radical, but ultimately unsuccessful, bid to win some kind of medal. In 1974, another group shot and killed twenty-two Israeli high school students at Ma'alot, near the

Lebanese border. Then in 1988, terrorists acting under the sponsorship of Libya's Colonel Gaddafi blew up an airliner over the Scottish village of Lockerbie, killing all 259 passengers and crew and eleven villagers.

The West reacted to these atrocities in differing ways. While the Israelis generally responded by driving tanks into Palestinian living rooms, Britain preferred to tackle the Lockerbie bombing in a more measured fashion, by putting one token suspect into a Scottish prison and then releasing him a few years later out of compassion. This, of course, caused a huge scandal, particularly when rumours emerged of a secret deal with Gaddafi in which top-level British officials had agreed to release al-Megrahi in return for the promise of seventy-two dark-eyed virgins in paradise.

There were also attempts to negotiate a peace settlement between Israel and Palestine. An agreement in Oslo in 1993 floundered upon the assassination of Yitzhak Rabin by Israeli fundamentalists. Another attempt by Bill Clinton at Camp David stalled when the Americans decided at the last minute to enlist the help of former president Carter, upon which eighteen high-ranking Hamas officials immediately blew themselves up.* Then, in 2002, President George Bush attempted to trick the Israelis and Palestinians into peace by forcing them to follow a road map, which, unbeknownst to either side, didn't lead anywhere. But a year later this had quickly reached a dead end too, and thus the fighting continues.

* With the full cooperation of the Israelis.

Al-Qaeda and the Taliban

On September 11th 2001, the world was stunned by the collision of two passenger jets with the Twin Towers of the World Trade Center in New York. At the moment it happened, President George Bush was visiting an elementary school in Florida, trying to learn to read. Nevertheless, as soon as he got to the end of his sentence some seven minutes later, he gained an immediate grasp of the situation. Two planes crashing into the same building on the same day? Bush knew it couldn't be a coincidence. 'They're flying too low!' he said to his startled chief of staff. 'That's why the planes are crashing. We need to get them to fly higher.'

Unfortunately, it turned out there was more to the story than that, and, as the long day unfolded, the world learned for the very first time the names Osama bin Laden and his chirpy backcrew al-Qaeda. Of course, if the world had been paying a bit more attention, it would have heard of these names a lot earlier, perhaps all the way back to the Soviet invasion of Afghanistan in 1979 which was when the Americans started supplying them with weapons. Since then, bin Laden and his bearded chums had launched attacks against American targets in Somalia, Yemen, East Africa and even the World Trade Center itself back in 1993. But nothing they had done even remotely rivalled the scale of September 11th. Clearly somebody needed to sort these jokers out before they started getting *really* ambitious.

Fortunately, Bush had a plan. Less than one month after the attacks, the US had chosen its first target: the Taliban. As its primary military strategy, the Pentagon ordered the CIA to supply weapons to a lawless band of Afghani extremists who would fight on their side, a move which caused a great deal of confusion inside CIA HQ Langley at first because they thought they already had. But it turned out this was a different lawless band of Afghani extremists than before, and on 12 November, with the Americans' help, the rampant Northern Alliance succeeding in taking Kabul, putting the evil Taliban on the run. Soon the country had a new provisional government under the leadership of Hamid Karzai, a man the Western allies knew they could trust to do a good job on account of his having a posh British accent.

All in all, things were going very well, and all that remained next was to find Osama bin Laden. Unfortunately, just as it looked as though the Western forces were on the right path, they found themselves sidetracked by the sudden and unexpected appearance of . . .

The Axis of Evil

With Afghanistan seemingly taken care of, Bush abruptly refocused his attention on the man who, along with bin Laden, the President and his coterie of neo-con advisers considered to be the greatest threat to world peace and the Western way of life: Al Gore. Believed to be the evil mastermind behind global warming, Mr Gore was never going to be an easy prey to catch, however. He was known to be a master of camouflage, with an uncanny ability to blend in with surrounding furniture and pot plants. In fact, some people reported being unable to see him even when he was standing right in front of them talking. Not surprisingly, the search for the ex-vice-president was unsuccessful and he still remains at large today.

Also still at large is the second prong of Bush's axis of evil: President Ahmadinejad of the Islamic Republic of Iran. A man never afraid of hearing his own voice, Ahmadinejad* has made no secret of his lofty ambitions for his country, his primary aspiration being to get it absolutely obliterated from the face of the planet. Thanks to a WikiLeaked diplomatic cable detailing the thoughts of the Saudi royal family, we now know how close he has come to achieving his dream:

* Correctly pronounced 'half-mad-on-jihad.'

> 22 Sept 2009: SECRET AND CONFIDENTIAL
> Spoke with King Abdullah. Saudis worried
> about Ahmadinejad's upcoming speech to UN.
> Will be so long, Irani nuclear programme
> may be completed by time f███ing thing
> ends. Recommends immediate annihilation of
> all Middle Eastern countries (█████ Saudi
> Arabia of course!). Also, continues to
> assure us that cousin Osama is definitely
> hiding somewhere in Afghan mountains.

The third and final prong was the late comic bad guy Kim Jong-il, leader of the Social People's Democratic Paradise of Korean Madmen. Laugh-a-minute Kim was a renowned practical joker in his home country, his favourite prank being to squander his nation's entire monetary resources on Mercedes-Benz with which, with perfect comic timing, he systematically ran over senior members of his staff. He also directed North Korea's elite scientists on a top-secret plan to manufacture thermo-nuclear weapons out of nothing but used toilet rolls and cling film. He regularly used this as a bargaining tool with the United States, whose intelligence agencies had alarmingly failed to predict the success of the project, not realising the North Koreans had anything as advanced as cling film. Despite these little foibles, the Dear Leader was hugely popular with his people, who regularly broke out in spontaneous mass expressions of carefully choreographed dancing.

Then on 17 December 2011 came a series of shock announcements on North Korea's state television.

2.30 Kim Jong poorly.

6.38 Kim Jong-il

9.00 Kim Jong-dead

This plunged his nation into mourning, and it was only the miraculous discovery of his heir Kim Jong-un on the divine slopes of Mount Paekdu that has given the North Korean people hope that they can continue toward their sacred destiny of total annihilation and death.

THE US AND UK PROVE THAT
SADDAM WAS STOCKPILING LETHAL
AMOUNTS OF SAND.

War in Iraq

As if President Ahmadinejad, Vice-President Gore, and Supreme Peerless Saviour of the Heavenly Revolution Kim Jong-il were not enough to be going on with, George Bush decided there was one more evil-doer he owed it to the world to dispose of, the West's old friend Saddam Hussein. His major motivation for doing so was that Saddam was, as the president put it, 'the guy who tried to kill my dad.' It was a statement that immediately put the rest of the world on edge, most particularly the Japanese whom, in the most significant act of his presidency, Bush Snr had memorably barfed upon after they poisoned him at a state dinner.

In addition to his personal reasons, Bush Jnr also argued that Saddam was concealing weapons of mass destruction, a claim that caused a great deal of scepticism in the governments of mainland Europe, who were sure they would have remembered selling them to him. To answer the growing number of critics, the Americans provided evidence of secret Iraqi hideaways in the desert in which Saddam was said to be stockpiling lethal amounts of sand. The Iraqi president was apparently planning to blow this evil yellow substance into the United States with the aid of a poisonous gas known as wind, which he was manufacturing in special mobile laboratories.

Fortunately, the Americans saw through his nefarious plot and invaded the country with their famous 'coalition of the countries who are scared of what we'll do if they don't'. Initially all went well, with American tanks rolling into Baghdad having barely had to kill a single British soldier. Statues of Saddam were toppled, and in May 2003 Bush felt confident enough to fly in triumph to the USS *Abraham Lincoln* aircraft carrier, where he famously declaimed to the cheering troops: 'Who's Abraham Lincoln?' But it soon transpired the president's move was premature. Despite the capture, trial and execution of Saddam, the violence continued and showed no signs of ending. Fortunately, the Americans and British decided to pull their troops out anyway.

Financial Armageddon

In September 2008, people all over the world turned on the news to find that everything they had ever worked for, all that they had spent their lives trying to create, was about to be vaporised by the actions of a few arrogant and irresponsible men. Fortunately, the Large Hadron Collider broke down before it could happen and people were able to turn their attention back to the collapse of the financial system. As the banks failed and stock markets plummeted, dazed men and women, wondering what had become of their hard-earned savings and retirement plans, staggered out on to the streets and looked up at the heavens, hoping to catch a glimpse of a stockbroker throwing himself out of a top-floor window.

But the stockbrokers simply walked out of the front door instead, claiming that they were the victims, not the perpetrators, of the crisis. The real perpetrators, it turned out, were the ranks of ordinary mortgage-holders stupid enough to have accepted loans from people whose brains were – it was quite clear now – made entirely of squashy pink mush. These mushy bankers now explained to the anxious world that they urgently required billions of dollars of taxpayer money in order to pay for the multimillion dollar bonuses they would need to award themselves for persuading the world their banks urgently required billions of dollars of taxpayer money. Still, nobody was able to get them to throw themselves out of a window.

Despite the widespread despair, the economic crisis did at least have one positive effect in terms of the election to the US presidency of Barack Obama.

The Chicago senator's victory marked, of course, an extraordinary watershed for both American politics and society as he became the first ever elected official in the nation's history who could dribble a basketball without falling over. He won the election by demanding 'change', by coincidence the same exact demand that was being made all over the world by homeless people whose houses the banks had just repossessed.

Although change has proved a bit harder to bring about than talk about, President Obama did score one significant victory in May 2011 when he personally tracked down Osama bin Laden to a modest high-walled mansion in Abbottabad, Pakistan. Assaulted by the heroic Seal Team Six, the West's arch-enemy was shot down in a room littered with dirty magazines and old porn, giving the world the final hopeful message that, despite centuries of conflict and distrust, men of all religions do have something important in common after all.

What next?

This, then, is the state of the world we live in now. It's not a pretty place, and I wouldn't advise going there. But what will the future hold? Will things improve for this beautiful planet of ours? Are we doomed to be incinerated by terrorist dirty bombs and broiled by global warming? Do we really care? These are questions perhaps only God can answer, if we can persuade Him to make a comeback.

But at least we can be certain of one thing, and in this lawless world it is not to be dismissed lightly. That is that no matter what mistakes the human race has made, no matter how destructive our reign on this planet has been and how appallingly we have behaved towards each other, we can hold our heads up high in one respect. We can say proudly and without fear of contradiction that at least the Earth is no longer being ruled by large flightless birds.

The End.